Alexander the Great

Alexander the Great

Other books in the Heroes and Villains series include:

King Arthur
Al Capone
Frederick Douglass
Adolf Hitler
Saddam Hussein
Martin Luther King Jr.
Josef Mengele
Oskar Schindler

Heroes and Villains

Alexander the Great

Louise Chipley Slavicek

LUCENT BOOKS

An imprint of Thomson Gale, a part of The Thomson Corporation

Detroit • New York • San Francisco • San Diego • New Haven, Conn. • Waterville, Maine • London • Munich

For Julie W. Chipley

© 2005 Thomson Gale, a part of The Thomson Corporation

Thomson and Star Logo are trademarks and Gale and Lucent Books are registered trademarks used herein under license.

For more information, contact
Lucent Books
27500 Drake Rd.
Farmington Hills, MI 48331-3535
Or you can visit our Internet site at http://www.gale.com

LIBRARY OF CONGRESS CATALOGING-IN-PUBLICATION DATA

Slavicek, Louise Chipley, 1956-
  Alexander the Great / by Louise Chipley Slavicek.
    p. cm. — (Heroes and villains)
  Includes bibliographical references and index.
  ISBN 1-59018-595-1 (hard cover : alk. paper)
  1. Alexander, the Great, 356-323 B.C.—Juvenile literature. 2. Greece—History—Macedonian Expansion, 359-323 B.C.—Juvenile literature. 3. Generals—Greece—Biography—Juvenile literature. 4. Greece—Kings and rulers—Biography—Juvenile literature. I. Title. II. Series.
  DF234.S59 2005
  938'.07'092—dc22   2004029133

Printed in the United States of America

Contents

Good and evil are an ever-present feature of human history. Their presence is reflected through the ages in tales of great heroism and extraordinary villainy. Such tales provide insight into human nature, whether they involve two people or two thousand, for the essence of heroism and villainy is found in deeds rather than in numbers. It is the deeds that pique our interest and lead us to wonder what prompts a man or woman to perform such acts.

Samuel Johnson, the eminent eighteenth-century English writer, once wrote, "The two great movers of the human mind are the desire for good, and fear of evil." The pairing of desire and fear, possibly two of the strongest human emotions, helps explain the intense fascination people have with all things good and evil—and by extension, heroic and villainous.

People are attracted to the person who reaches into a raging river to pull a child from what could have been a watery grave for both, and to the person who risks his or her own life to shepherd hundreds of desperate black slaves to safety on the Underground Railroad. We wonder what qualities these heroes possess that enable them to act against self-interest, and even their own survival. We also wonder if, under similar circumstances, we would behave as they do.

Evil, on the other hand, horrifies as well as intrigues us. Few people can look upon the drifter who mutilates and kills a neighbor or the dictator who presides over the torture and murder of thousands of his own citizens without feeling a sense of revulsion. And yet, as Joseph Conrad writes, we experience "the fascination of the abomination." How else to explain the overwhelming success of a book such as Truman Capote's *In Cold Blood*, which examines in horrifying detail a vicious and senseless murder that took place in the American heartland in the 1960s? The popularity of murder mysteries and Court TV are also evidence of the human fascination with villainy.

Most people recoil in the face of such evil. Yet most feel a deep-seated curiosity about the kind of person who could commit a terrible act. It is perhaps a reflection of our innermost fears that we wonder whether we could resist or stand up to such behavior in our presence or even if we ourselves possess the capacity to commit such terrible crimes.

The Lucent Books Heroes and Villains series capitalizes on our fascination with the perpetrators of both good and evil by introducing readers to some of history's most revered heroes and hated villains. These include heroes such as Frederick Douglass, who knew firsthand the humiliation of slavery and, at great risk to himself, publicly fought to abolish the institution of slavery in America. It also includes villains such as Adolf Hitler, who is remembered both for the devastation of Europe and for the murder of 6 million Jews and thousands of Gypsies, Slavs, and others whom Hitler deemed unworthy of life.

Each book in the Heroes and Villains series examines the life story of a hero or villain from history. Generous use of primary and secondary source quotations gives readers eyewitness views of the life and times of each individual as well as enlivens the narrative. Notes and annotated bibliographies provide stepping-stones to further research.

Alexander the Great, Hero or Villain?

The brief reign of Alexander the Great lasted just over a dozen years (336–323 B.C.). Yet by the time of his death at age thirty-two, the young king had created the greatest empire the world had ever known, stretching from Greece and Egypt in the west to modern-day Afghanistan and Pakistan in the east. Although the epic scale of his accomplishments is beyond dispute, over the nearly twenty-four hundred years since Alexander's death, opinion has been sharply divided regarding the conqueror's fundamental character and intentions.

Unquestionably, Alexander the Great is not only one of the most famous figures in world history but also one of the most controversial. Over the millennia, Alexander has been viewed as both a hero and a villain—a benevolent liberator and a ruthless conqueror, an inspiring leader and an alcoholic tyrant, a visionary promoter of the brotherhood of humankind and a cold-blooded murderer responsible for the deaths of hundreds of thousands of innocent people.

Judging Alexander the Great

One reason for the profound disagreement concerning Alexander the Great's character and motives is the nature of the existing source material. Virtually all of the evidence for Alexander's life and career comes from works composed long after his reign. A number of Alexander's contemporaries, including several of his leading generals, penned detailed accounts of the king during the period immediately following his death. Unfortunately, these contemporary chronicles were lost and the only knowledge of them comes from their use by a small group of Greek and Roman historians who lived hundreds of years after Alexander. The earliest of these historians, Diodorus Siculus, wrote his account of Alexander the Great in the mid–first century B.C., almost exactly three centuries after the conqueror's death. Arrian, Plutarch, and Quintus Curtius Rufus—Alexander's other chief ancient biographers—composed their chronicles during the first and second centuries A.D.

In addition to the limitations of the source material, another explanation for the widely differing assessments of Alexander's basic character and aims can be found in the personal biases and assumptions of his admirers and critics. Inevitably, contemporary values and attitudes have influenced evaluations of the famed ruler. For example, shaped by a culture that glorified military prowess and empire building, most ancient Roman commentators deeply admired Alexander for his strategic and tactical brilliance on the battlefield as well as the sheer scope of his conquests. Medieval Europeans, living in a society that extolled warfare and the chivalric code, also portrayed Alexander the Great in glowing terms, romanticizing him as the ideal knight, the most honorable, brave, and skillful warrior of all time.

Modern scholars, however, have tended to see Alexander the Great and his exploits in a very different light. In an

Julius Caesar pays homage before the body of Alexander the Great in the conqueror's tomb.

age when warfare and violent conquest are far more likely to be decried than exalted, late-twentieth- and early twenty-first-century historians have stressed the high price in suffering and blood that Alexander's military campaigns exacted from the peoples he vanquished. To many modern historians, Alexander is not the dashing, heroic warrior-king of the ancient Roman or medieval chronicles but, rather, a brutal, power-hungry invader, a bringer of destruction, despair, and death to thousands of Persians, Indians, and other peoples.

Alexander the Great and his remarkable career of conquest have always been viewed in different ways; his nobility or depravity is truly in the eyes of the beholder. Yet praised or censured, admired or reviled, Alexander has remained one of the most studied individuals in world history. Today, nearly twenty-four centuries since his death, Alexander the Great is as much an object of fascination as ever, not only because of what he accomplished during his brief reign but also because of what this complex and enigmatic leader is perceived to be—hero or villain, or perhaps a bit of both.

Chapter One

A Warrior-King in Training

Sometime in July 356 B.C.—the exact date is unknown—a son was born to King Philip II of Macedon and his wife Queen Olympias. The boy, whom Philip and Olympias named Alexander, would come to reflect many of his strong-willed parents' characteristics, both positive and negative. The rough and warlike society in which the crown prince grew up would also play a vital role in molding his character, values, and aspirations. Alexander the Great was as much a product of fourth-century B.C. Macedon as he was of his heredity.

Macedon and Greece

Alexander's homeland lay in the rugged far northeastern reaches of the Greek peninsula. Yet even though the ancient Macedonians worshipped the Greek gods, spoke a form of Greek, and insisted that their kings were of Greek descent, the Macedonians' neighbors to the south tended to view them as outsiders, and backward ones at that. The kingdom of Macedon, writes historian Richard Stoneman, "was an oddity in the Greek world."[1] Central and southern Greece was a patchwork of small, self-ruling city-states. During the two centuries before Alexander's birth, most of the city-states embarked on a great political experiment, abandoning their traditional monarchies for democracies in which power was shared by a large portion of the (male) citizenry. Macedon, in contrast, did not fragment into a host of independent city-states. Nor did it develop democratic political institutions. As of 356 B.C., when Alexander was born, Macedon remained a large territorial state ruled by an absolute monarch.

Macedon's more centralized structure and monarchical form of government were not the only things that made it an "oddity" within the Greek world. The kingdom's neighbors to the south also regarded Macedon's social customs and mores as alien and backward. To Athenians, Thebans, and other mainland Greeks, notes one historian, "the Macedonians were barbarian, half wild."[2] Because of the northerners' rough ways, and especially the behavior of their "hard-living court," who apparently valued fighting, hunting, and carousing over intellectual debate or the theater, many Greeks judged the Macedonians as unworthy "to be called Hellenes, that is true bearers of Greek civilization,"[3] writes scholar Michael Wood.

Above all, the Greeks looked down on Alexander's countrymen for their drinking habits. Greeks traditionally diluted their wine with water. Macedonians, in contrast, drank their alcohol full strength and in quantities that horrified their neighbors. According to one Greek observer, the Macedonians were a people who "never understood how to drink in moderation."[4] Philip and his nobles guzzled so much wine at the beginning of a banquet, he

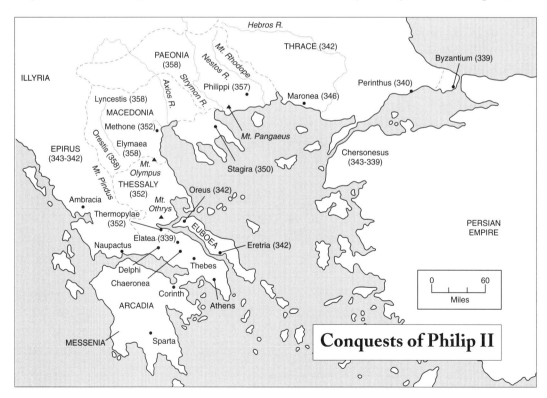

Conquests of Philip II

claimed, that they were drunk before the first course arrived. The king and his wine-swilling courtiers might have proudly traced their nation's origins from Macedon, the legendary half-human son of the Greek god Zeus, but their supposed kinsmen in Athens and Thebes remained unconvinced. Since the ancient Greeks firmly believed that "moderation was the hallmark of the civilized [and] drunkenness . . . the way of the barbarian,"[5] explains Alexander biographer John Maxwell O'Brien, for many Greeks, the Macedonians' drinking habits made them appear all the more as uncouth foreigners.

King Philip and the Rise of Macedon

The people of Athens and the other Greek city-states might have disdained their neighbors for what they deemed the Macedonians' uncouth ways, but by the time of Alexander's birth, "barbaric" Macedon was rapidly becoming the leading military and political power on the Greek peninsula. And the driving force behind Macedon's remarkable rise to prominence in the mid–fourth century B.C. was none other than Alexander's father, King Philip.

When the twenty-four-year-old Philip came to the throne in 359 B.C., Macedon was militarily feeble and hemmed in by hostile and expansive neighbors to the north, east, and west. The new king was determined to reorganize his army into a formidable

King Philip of Macedon transformed the weak Macedonian army into a formidable machine of war.

fighting machine on which Macedon could rely in its ongoing struggles against the Paeonians and Thracians to the kingdom's north and east and the Illyrian tribes to its west. Immediately after assuming power, Philip began transforming the royal forces from a weak, undisciplined group into a superbly trained body of warriors armed with the latest weaponry, most notably the *sarissa*, a sixteen-foot, iron-tipped pike that was more than twice as long as the average spear of the era.

The key component of Philip's new and improved army was the *sarissa*-wielding infantry phalanx, highly trained foot soldiers who advanced in long rows bearing their gigantic pikes horizontally so that their terrified opponents found themselves confronted by a slanting, virtually impenetrable wall of iron spikes.

By mid-356 B.C., when Alexander first arrived on the scene, Philip had managed to use Macedon's revitalized army not only to crush his Paeonian and Illyrian neighbors but also to conquer much of Thessaly, which bordered Macedon on the southeast, and several Athenian colonies on the northern Aegean coast. Over the next decade and a half, Philip would expand Macedon's territory and influence further by claiming all of Thessaly as well as Thrace, a vast region that is now split among the modern nations of Bulgaria, Greece, and Turkey. Under Philip's energetic leadership, Macedon was well on its way to becoming the foremost power in southern Europe.

The Education of Alexander

From earliest childhood, Alexander was groomed for the day when he would become master of the empire his father had created. Although Alexander's mother, Olympias, was the polygamous Philip's third wife, she was the first—and for many years the only—of his spouses to produce a son. (Polygamy, the practice of having more than one spouse at the same time was a tradition among the Macedonian royalty.) As Philip's heir apparent, young Alexander was carefully trained and educated to be a Macedonian warrior-king in the tradition of his illustrious father.

At the age of seven Alexander was considered old enough to begin his formal education. His first tutor was Leonidas, a kinsman of Olympias. Alexander learned to read and write Greek and play the lyre (a harplike instrument), skills that were considered essential for a Macedonian nobleman. Leonidas seems to have placed more emphasis on the prince's physical development than on his literary or musical instruction, however. A harsh taskmaster, he compelled his young charge to follow a grueling program of exercise and self-denial. According to the Greek historian Plutarch, Alexander later recalled that Leonidas considered a light breakfast as a fitting reward for a long night of marching, and his idea of supper was a small meal based on rations. To ensure that his young pupil remained faithful to this spartan regimen, Leonidas even rummaged through "the chests where I kept my bedding and clothing," Alexander reportedly complained, "to make sure my mother hadn't put some delicacy . . . in there."[6] The adult Alexander seems to have harbored more than a little resentment toward his earliest mentor. Nonetheless, notes historian A.B. Bosworth, the remarkable "capacity for hardship and physical exertion" the conqueror exhibited during his military campaigns probably owed much to "the rigorous physical discipline"[7] that Alexander was subjected to as a boy.

Few details regarding the prince's military training have survived. As part of Alexander's preparation to become a great warrior-king like his father, he must have received extensive instruction in both horsemanship and the use of weapons, such as the sword, the bow, the javelin, and the notorious *sarissa*. Above all, Alexander's teachers would have instilled in him the fundamental code of the Macedonian soldier: For a man, "Glory in war was life's highest honor."[8] As Alexander the Great's remarkable military career amply testifies, it was a lesson that the young warrior-king in training learned well.

Alexander, Aristotle, and Achilles

To cap the future monarch's education, when Alexander was thirteen Philip invited the renowned Greek philosopher Aristotle to Macedon to tutor his son. For the next three years, Alexander studied with this illustrious teacher at the village of Mieza near Pella, Macedon's capital, while continuing his military training in the company of other aristocratic boys his age. One of the prince's companions at Mieza was a young Macedonian noble named Hephaestion. Until Hephaestion's death in Persia two decades later, he would remain Alexander's closest friend.

It is generally assumed that Alexander developed his lifelong interest in scientific investigation as a student of Aristotle. The Greek philosopher was an authority on all the sciences, including astronomy, biology, zoology, medicine, and geography, as well as being an expert on political theory. Aristotle also seems to have instilled an enduring appreciation for Greek culture in his pupil. In later years, Alexander the Great became a generous patron of Greek artists, musicians, and authors.

In the realm of literature, Aristotle deepened young Alexander's already strong appreciation for Homer's famous poem about the legendary Trojan War, the *Iliad*. According to Greek tradition, Homer, who is thought to have lived sometime during the eighth century B.C., was the first and greatest Greek poet. From earliest childhood, Alexander had been drawn to Homer's epic account of the Greek siege of Troy (on the coast of modern Turkey) to avenge the kidnapping of the beautiful Spartan princess, Helen. Throughout his life, Alexander would regard an edited version of the poem that Aristotle presented to him at Mieza as one of his most prized possessions. According to Plutarch, the conqueror carried his annotated version of the *Iliad* with him everywhere he went, even keeping the book "under his pillow along with his dagger"[9] while he slept.

A Budding Scientist

Historians generally credit Alexander's three years of study with Aristotle at Mieza with inspiring the teenager to develop into an inquiring scientist, as this excerpt from Robin Lane Fox's Alexander the Great *illustrates.*

[A] boy could not help learning curiosity from Aristotle, and to fourteen-year-old Alexander, he would seem less the abstract philosopher than the man who knew the ways of a cuttlefish, who could tell why wrynecks [a kind of bird] had a tongue or how hedgehogs would mate standing up, who had practiced vivisection on a tortoise and had described the life cycle of an Aegean mosquito. Medicine, animals, the lie of the land and the shape of the seas; these were interests which Aristotle could communicate and Philip had already instanced [displayed], and each was a part of adult Alexander. He prescribed cures for snakebite to his friends; he suggested that a new strain of cattle should be shipped from India to Macedonia; he shared his father's interest in drainage and irrigation and the reclaiming of waste land; his surveyors paced out the roads in Asia, and his fleet was detailed to explore the Caspian Sea and the Indian ocean; his treasurer experimented with European plants in a Babylonian garden, and thanks to the expedition's findings, Aristotle's most intelligent pupil could include the banyan, the cinnamon and a bush of myrrh in books which mark the beginnings of botany [the study of plants]. Alexander was more than a man of ambition and toughness; he had the wide armory of interests of a man of curiosity, and in the days at Mieza there had been matter enough to arouse them.

Under the tutelage of Aristotle (left), Alexander (right) developed a keen interest in scientific study.

For Alexander, as for many ancient Greeks, the *Iliad* and its sequel, the *Odyssey*, were more than great works of literature; they were also moral guidebooks. And the fundamental rules of conduct that the poems stressed—and their legendary hero Achilles embodied—were the same code that Alexander's warrior-king father and Macedonian tutors had drilled into him throughout his boyhood: A man could achieve no higher honor in this world than distinction in battle.

To Prince Alexander, Achilles was the very model of heroic virtue. At the climax of Achilles' saga, the Greek warrior slays his chief Trojan adversary in one-on-one combat even though he has been forewarned that killing his enemy would bring about his own demise. A devoted champion of his own and his homeland's honor, writes O'Brien,

Achilles deliberately chose "a glorious early death" on the battlefield over "a long but uneventful life."[10] In one of the most famous passages in the *Iliad*, Achilles relates the conditions of the choice confronting him: "My goddess mother says that two possible destinies bear me toward the end of life. If I remain to fight at Troy I lose my homecoming, but my fame will be eternal. Or if I return to my dear home, I lose that glorious fame, but a long life awaits me."[11] In common with his beloved hero, Alexander would also boldly pursue "eternal fame" in military conquest only to die young, far from his home.

Alexander and His Mother

Alexander's devotion to Achilles and his epic saga was strongly encouraged by his high-strung and eccentric mother, Olympias. Olympias, a member of the

Alexander was fascinated with the exploits of the Greek hero Achilles, shown here (center) in battle. To Alexander, Achilles personified heroic virtue and honor.

According to some accounts, Olympias (background) convinced Alexander that Zeus was his father.

not only the descendant of the Greek world's most celebrated hero but also the offspring of its most powerful god, Zeus. Greek tradition held that Zeus would occasionally leave the realm of the gods and disguise himself in order to seduce some mortal woman he fancied. Several of these women were said to have borne him children, including the Spartan queen Leda, whose liaison with Zeus produced the legendary Helen of Homer's *Iliad*. The account of his conception that Olympias allegedly confided to Alexander was that Zeus, in the guise of a snake, had impregnated her one night while she slept. Plutarch, however, claims that some of his sources doubted this story, maintaining that Olympias was far too religious to have concocted such an outrageous tale about the king of the gods. Whenever she was asked about the rumor in later years, Olympias reportedly insisted that the goddess Hera—Zeus's wife—would never have forgiven her for telling such a wicked falsehood.

royal family of Epirus, a mountainous region to the west of Macedon, proudly counted the legendary Greek champion among her ancestors. Consequently, young Alexander grew up with the cherished belief that he was a direct descendant of his supreme hero.

According to some ancient accounts, Olympias may have attempted to persuade Alexander that he was

Indeed, although much about Olympias remains a mystery, there is no question that she was an intensely religious woman. In the ancient Greek world there was a long-standing tradition for women to form cults honoring Dionysus, the god of wine and spiritual possession, and Olympias had a reputation for being one of Dionysus's most ardent disciples. According to author David Sacks, members of these all-female religious cults believed they could commune directly with Dionysus through a "divinely inspired frenzy" in which their own "human personality briefly vanished, supposedly replaced by the identity of the god."[12] Writes Plutarch of the queen:

> Olympias, it is said, outdid the other women in her efforts to achieve possession by the god and used to exhibit her inspiration in a wilder fashion: she would introduce great tame snakes into the meetings, which used to terrify the men [who were observing] by crawling out of the . . . ritual baskets and coiling themselves around the women's wands and garlands.[13]

The passionately religious Olympias was a dominant force in her son's early years. Certainly, Olympias's influence on Alexander's religious beliefs appears to have been profound. Throughout his life, Alexander "exhibited a strong penchant [bent] for oracles, cults and omens," writes Wood, "which we might guess he inherited from his mother, along with her volatile and emotional temperament."[14] Following the example set by Olympias, the adult Alexander dutifully honored the gods every day with sacrifices and other rites, showing particular respect to the supreme deity Zeus.

Alexander and His Father

According to most accounts, the crown prince and his mother were devoted to each other. In contrast, young Alexander's relationship with his father was often strained. At the heart of the trouble between Philip and the boy seems to have been Alexander's fiercely competitive and ambitious nature.

Plutarch reports that Alexander the Great's "ambitious desire for recognition"[15] was the driving force in his life even as a young child. Yet, as one of Alexander's modern biographers notes, it "was no small task to become great when measured against Philip of Macedon."[16] News of Philip's military conquests, rather than filling Alexander with pride for his father's achievements, filled him with dread that he would never be able to match his feats. After hearing that the king had captured yet another powerful and wealthy city, Alexander supposedly complained to his friends, "Lads, my father's going to pre-empt me in everything. By the time he's finished, there'll be nothing important left for me to present to the world, no splendid victories to be won."[17]

Resolved not only to equal but to surpass his warrior-king father, Alexander seized every opportunity he could to outdo Philip. The most famous anecdote from Alexander's childhood, the story of the prince and the horse Bucephalas, illustrates the boy's fierce determination to surpass his illustrious parent by achieving something his father could not—or dared not—do. When Alexander was about nine years old, Philip was offered a handsome black stallion. No one had ever been able to mount the horse, and after observing the stallion's erratic behavior with his grooms, Philip commanded that the animal be taken away "on the grounds that he was . . . uncontrollable," Plutarch reports. As the stallion was being led away, Alexander burst out, "What a horse they are losing! And all because they are too inexperienced and feeble to manage him!" Philip's response was swift and angry: "Who are you to criticize your elders?" he snapped. "'Do you think you . . . can manage horses better?' . . . 'Yes,' Alexander boldly replied, 'I do think I could manage *this* horse better than others have done.'"[18]

Amid much laughter from his father and the other onlookers, Alexander ran to the rearing stallion and, taking hold of his reins, "turned him to face the sun—apparently because he had noticed that the horse was made jittery by the sight of his shadow stretching out and jerking in front of him," writes Plutarch. While Philip, by now deeply alarmed for his son's safety, watched with bated breath, Alexander mounted the horse and galloped across the field. After the prince "made a perfect turn and started back jubilant and triumphant," Philip, awed by the boy's daring, reputedly declared, "Son, you had better try to find a kingdom you fit: Macedonia is too small for you."[19] Bucephalas, as

Alexander named the stallion, would become the conqueror's favorite war-horse, carrying his master into nearly all of his battles until its death in modern-day Pakistan some twenty years after the young prince had tamed him.

Early Military Triumphs

The self-assurance, daring, and independence of mind that Alexander displayed in breaking Bucephalas would serve the prince well several years later when his father put him in charge of Macedon while he was away on a military campaign. Although Alexander was just sixteen years old at the time, Philip had sufficient confidence in his strong-willed son to name him as his deputy.

No sooner had Philip and his army departed than the Maedi, a warlike tribe who lived on Macedon's northern frontiers, launched a revolt against their Macedonian overlords. Alexander eagerly accepted the challenge, setting out at once for southern Thrace, the heart of Maedi country. There, in an impressive display of military skill, the prince and his troops routed the tribesmen and seized their capital city. After resettling the capital with Macedonian soldiers and citizens as a military colony, Alexander proudly dubbed it Alexandropolis, in imitation of the outpost Philippopolis that had been founded by his father in Thrace two years earlier. As it turned out, Alexandropolis was to be the first of dozens of cities on three different continents that Alexander would name after himself.

A young Alexander tames the wild stallion Bucephalas. Impressed with Alexander's daring in breaking the intractable horse, Philip predicted a great future for his son.

Alexander's Striking Physical Presence

Most of the ancient sources on Alexander agree that the conqueror's physical appearance was arresting. Like the famous French military and political leader Napoleon, Alexander the Great was short—perhaps not much over five feet tall—with a muscular build. Although his thick, flowing hair was often compared to a lion's mane, his beard was so sparse that he chose to go clean-shaven, despite the fact that Macedonian noblemen traditionally sported full beards. Alexander's complexion "was pale ... and used to take on a ruddy tinge especially around the chest and face," writes Plutarch. His skin, he adds, emitted "a delightful odour and ... his mouth and whole body used to be bathed in a fragrance which filled his clothes. This was perhaps due to the unusually hot and fiery blend of the humors in his body." Reflecting popular medical ideas of the early second century A.D. when he was writing, Plutarch concluded that it was almost certainly "the heat of Alexander's body ... which gave him his fondness for drink and also made him impatient."

Alexander, whose eyes were of different colors—one dark brown and one gray-blue—possessed a "melting gaze," according to Plutarch, and an unusual habit of tilting his head upward and slightly to the left. These traits have prompted some modern medical experts to conclude that Alexander suffered from a rare disorder of the optic muscles known as Brown's syndrome, in which the eyes do not move together properly. If this diagnosis is correct, Alexander probably bent his head upward and to one side in order to avoid double vision.

As this bust shows, Alexander was a handsome man with a striking appearance.

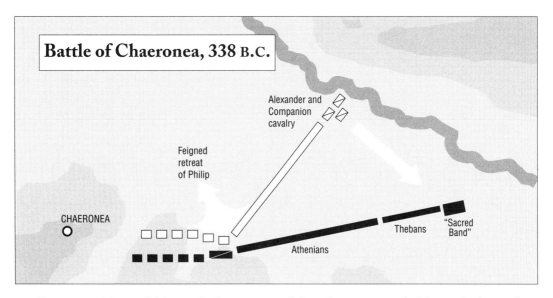

Battle of Chaeronea, 338 B.C.

Alexander and Companion cavalry

Feigned retreat of Philip

CHAERONEA

Thebans

"Sacred Band"

Athenians

In recognition of Alexander's victory against the Maedi, Philip honored the teenager with the rank of general. The following year, in 338 B.C. eighteen-year-old Alexander took part in a full-scale battle when the Macedonian army confronted an allied Greek force led by Athens and Thebes near Chaeronea in central Greece. Over the past two decades, Philip had been steadily increasing his control over the city-states of the Greek peninsula. The Battle of Chaeronea represented their last desperate bid for independence from Macedonian domination.

At Chaeronea, Philip placed Alexander in command of the army's elite mounted unit, the companion cavalry. Noting a break in the Greek line, Alexander lost no time in leading a bold charge against Thebes's famous crack forces, the Sacred Band. Chaeronea ended in a resounding victory for the Macedonians, and Alexander's performance in the battle earned him acclaim for his courage and his adeptness at seizing the moment, a gift that would prove to be a hallmark of Alexander the Great's long military career.

Chaeronea signified the death of Greek independence. Soon after the battle, a Panhellenic (united Greek) coalition, the League of Corinth, was organized under Philip's leadership, "a polite way of indicating that Philip now controlled Greece,"[20] notes Stoneman. The daring and tactical shrewdness Alexander displayed at the decisive clash near Chaeronea made Philip extremely proud of his son, Plutarch asserts. Nonetheless, Philip's treatment of Alexander's beloved mother Olympias would soon drive a wedge between father and son. For a time, it even appeared that Alexander might not inherit the kingship for which he had spent nearly his entire life preparing.

Chapter Two

INHERITING HIS FATHER'S THRONE

As he stood on the brink of adulthood, Prince Alexander had good reason to fear that the crown he had always viewed as his birthright might never be his. When an unexpected turn of events left the twenty-year-old in charge of his father's vast realm, Alexander moved quickly to consolidate his position at home and throughout the Greek world. In doing so, the new king revealed a capacity for ruthlessness and brutality that he was to display time and time again during the course of his career.

A Devastating Family Quarrel

With Athens and the other Greek city-states vanquished at the Battle of Chaeronea, King Philip had become the most powerful ruler on the European continent. But all was not well in the royal palace at Pella. Although Olympias had never been Philip's sole wife, since leaving her native Epirus to marry him some twenty years earlier, she had been the most influential and esteemed of the king's various spouses (who numbered at least five as of the summer of 338 B.C. when the Battle of Chaeronea was fought). A few months after his victory at Chaeronea, however, all that changed when Philip fell in love with a young Macedonian woman named Cleopatra. Olympias had always had plenty of rivals for her husband's affection, but Cleopatra was different. The niece of Philip's trusted general Attalus, Cleopatra was a part of one of Macedonia's oldest and most important families. After announcing their betrothal, the adoring Philip even honored his blue-blooded Macedonian fiance with the name Eurydice, the name of his mother. Olympias felt both humiliated and threatened by Philip's newest marriage, and Alexander loyally took his cherished mother's side in the growing rift between his parents.

The escalating tension between father and son came to a head at Philip and Eurydice's wedding banquet, writes Stoneman, "which as usual in Macedonian festivities involved massive consumption of strong wine."[21] According to Plutarch, a drunken Attalus loudly called on his fellow Macedonians to pray that Philip and his niece would be blessed with a legitimate heir to their homeland's throne. Whether Attalus intended to imply that Alexander was an unsuitable heir to the kingship because his mother was not a native Macedonian or was actually accusing the prince of being illegitimate is unclear. Either way, Alexander was incensed and impetuously hurled his wine goblet at the general's head. Philip, whose drinking was notorious, responded to what in his inebriated condition he apparently viewed as the teenager's impertinence by drawing his sword and lunging at his own son. Alexander escaped unscathed when the king stumbled over a couch and ended up sprawled face first on the floor.

The next morning, Alexander and his mother left Macedon in a huff, with Olympias heading for her native land of Epirus and Alexander for nearby Illyria.

Alexander's self-imposed exile was destined to be short-lived, for father and son soon reconciled. Nonetheless, Alexander returned home with the knowledge that his once rock-solid standing as Philip's heir remained in grave jeopardy. Both Alexander and Olympias were well aware that under Macedonian tradition, kings with more than one male child did not necessarily have to be succeeded by their eldest son. Therefore, when Eurydice gave birth to a baby boy named Caranus early in the summer of 336 B.C., Alexander's future appeared more uncertain than ever.

"Such Was the End of Philip"

Whether Alexander had any role in what happened next will probably never be known, but there can be no doubt that he was in a vulnerable position by the summer of 336 B.C. That July the entire royal family, including Olympias, assembled in the old Macedonian capital of Aegae to celebrate the wedding of Alexander's sister. On the second day of the festivities, athletic competitions were slated to take place at Aegae's stadium. Having ordered his bodyguards to follow him at a slight distance, Philip made his grand entrance into the arena alone. Suddenly a man rushed toward the king and stabbed him in the chest. The assassin, a young aristocrat named Pausanias, was tackled and slain on the spot by several Macedonian noblemen. But the forty-seven-year-old ruler had

Many historians believe Olympias played a key role in the assassination of King Philip.

They believed that Philip's spurned wife Olympias had a hand in the assassination. Olympias, her accusers pointed out, had much to gain from the death of the man who had humiliated her and whose removal while his new son was still an infant would almost surely result in the crowning of her own child, Alexander, as king. Many modern scholars agree. Indeed, contends Peter Green, Olympias's behavior after the assassination "suggests that she not only planned her husband's death but openly gloried in it."[23] Immediately after Philip's death, the slain Pausanias's body was nailed to a gibbet (a gallows with a projecting arm for suspending and displaying the corpses of executed criminals). According to some ancient sources, that same night Olympias crowned Pausanias with a gold wreath. Several days later, she ordered that the body be taken down from the gibbet and given a proper burial. Every year on the anniversary of Philip's murder, it was said, Olympias would make a ceremony of pouring libations at the spot where Pausanias's corpse had once hung. (In the ancient Greek world, libations involved the pouring of wine or another liquid in honor of a deity.)

already succumbed to his wounds. "Such was the end of Philip, who had made himself the greatest of the kings in Europe in his time,"[22] writes the Greek historian Diodorus.

The murderer's precise motives remain a mystery. The one surviving contemporary account of the killer claims that Pausanias had a personal grudge against the king and his general and kinsman by marriage, Attalus. Some Macedonians, however, suspected that Pausanias had not acted alone.

Although none of the ancient sources accuse the prince of conspiring in his father's assassination, a few modern historians have implicated not only Olympias but also Alexander himself in Philip's death. Those who accuse

Alexander of plotting against his father stress the way in which the murderer was handled. No effort whatsoever seems to have been made to take Pausanias alive. Instead, a small group of Macedonian noblemen ran the assassin through with spears as Pausanias tried to flee the stadium for the nearby city gate, where he had a horse waiting. The fact that every one of these noblemen happened to be a close friend of Alexander's has caused some scholars to speculate that Alexander may have put his comrades up to killing the unsuspecting Pausanias in order to silence his co-conspirator in Philip's murder.

It cannot be denied that the king's death came at an opportune moment for his eldest son. Yet, as historian Robin Lane Fox points out, whether "Alexander could ever have brought himself to connive at Philip's murder is a question which only faith or prejudice can pretend to answer; they had quarreled . . . [but] there is no evidence to prove that he hated Philip's memory, let alone that he claimed credit for his death."[24] Moreover, observe Alan Fildes

A Royal Tomb

In 1977 the Greek archaelogist Manolis Andronicos made a dramatic find near the old Macedonian capital of Aegae (modern Vergina): a vast, vaulted tomb dating to the fourth century B.C. The tomb, which had somehow escaped being plundered by grave robbers, contained a number of magnificent and rare objects, including a crown of golden oak leaves, gold-plated greaves (long armor plates that shield the shins), silver and gold wine vessels, and three miniature ivory heads that appeared to represent Philip II, his wife Olympias, and son Alexander. In the middle of the tomb was a golden sarcophagus (coffin) exquisitely decorated with a starburst, the emblem of the Macedonian royal house.

On opening the sarcophagus, Andronicos discovered the remains of a man in his mid- to late forties wrapped in a sumptuous purple cloth. On the skull there was evidence of a massive wound across the right eye, the same eye in which Alexander the Great's father was supposed to have been blinded by an enemy arrow. Although there is much compelling evidence that the grave uncovered by Andronicos holds the remains of Philip II, some archaeologists believe that the tomb belonged to a later Macedonian king (but not Alexander, who was buried in Egypt). Since no identifying inscriptions have ever been found at the site, however, the question of whose remains were entombed at Aegae will probably never be answered once and for all.

and Joann Fletcher, given Alexander's religious faith, "such a calculated act as patricide [the act of killing one's father]—the most serious crime in the eyes of the gods—would have been totally out of character for the prince."[25]

Alexander Moves to Secure His Father's Throne

Immediately after Philip's assassination, Antipater, one of the slain ruler's top generals, presented Alexander to an assembly of Macedon's warrior nobility for acclamation as their new king in accordance with Macedonian custom. That a majority of the assembly promptly hailed the twenty-year-old as their new leader is not surprising: Alexander's successful campaign against the rebellious Maedi and his courageous and skillful performance at the Battle of Chaeronea two years later had already won him the respect of his country's military elite. To allay the concerns of those who thought he was too young or inexperienced for his awesome new responsibilities, Alexander assured the royal army that the government of Macedon was changing in name alone, for he would strive to follow his father's example in all things.

Despite the ease with which he had gained the backing of most of Macedon's warrior nobility, Alexander worried that his position was not secure. His first task as King Alexander III was to direct the investigation into Philip's

assassination. Alexander used the opportunity to liquidate all those whom he suspected of coveting his throne. The first to die were two popular princes from Lyncestis, a fiercely independent district in Macedon's hill country. Although Alexander officially charged the men with conspiring with Pausanias to murder Philip, the new king could well "have had other reasons for their elimination,"[26] suggests O'Brien. Years earlier, the Argead dynasty (ruling house) to which Philip and Alexander belonged had struggled for control of Macedon with the Lyncestian royal family. Alexander may have feared that the princes could become dangerous rivals if the Lyncestians, who had never reconciled themselves to Argead rule, rallied behind the two as the legitimate successors to the Macedonian crown.

After disposing of the Lyncestian princes, Alexander next turned his attention to his twenty-five-year-old cousin Amyntas. The son of Philip's older brother and predecessor as king of Macedon, Amyntas was still a toddler when his father died in battle. Although Amyntas had been designated as his father's regent, impressed by Philip's successes on the battlefield, Macedon's warrior nobility decided to bypass the child altogether and acclaim Philip as their ruler instead. In light of Amyntas's history, Alexander could not help but view his older cousin as a potential competitor for the throne. Like Alexander's Lyncestian rivals,

Alexander Pays a Visit to Diogenes

According to several ancient accounts, while Alexander was traveling through central Greece in late 336 B.C., he encountered the celebrated Greek philosopher Diogenes. Diogenes was a follower of the Cynic school of thought, a philosophy that stressed the pursuit of virtue as the chief aim of human existence. According to the Cynics, the wise man or woman is one who shuns all worldly pleasures and honors for a life of poverty and seclusion. Diogenes became famous throughout Greece for taking these principles to an extreme: It was said that he subsisted on water and the coarsest bread and made his home in a clay tub.

Supposedly, Alexander spotted Diogenes sunning himself near his tub one day while the king and his entourage were touring the city of Corinth. Alexander politely asked the famed philosopher if he could do anything for him. Diogenes snapped that he could move a bit to the side, for Alexander was blocking his sun. According to Plutarch, Alexander was so impressed by the philosopher's "haughty detachment, that while the members of his retinue were ridiculing and mocking Diogenes as they left, he said, 'But as for me, if I were not Alexander, I would be Diogenes.'" Peter Green in his *Alexander of Macedon, 356–323 B.C.*, writes,

> [Alexander's comment showed] shrewd percipience [keen discernment]. Both men shared (and surely recognized in each other) the same quality of stubborn and alienated intransigence [willfulness]. But whereas Diogenes had withdrawn from the world, Alexander was bent on subjugating it: they represented the active and passive forms of an identical phenomenon. It is not surprising, in the circumstances, that their encounter should have been so abrasive.

Amyntas was found guilty of treason and summarily executed.

Alexander's role in the death of his cousin Amyntas is beyond dispute. Historians disagree, however, regarding Alexander's culpability for the murder of his young half-brother, Caranus. Some scholars like Richard Stoneman believe that Alexander, fearful that the boy could become a focus for rebellion in the future, expressly ordered Olympias to kill Philip and Eurydice's infant son while he was away from Pella on a military campaign. In contrast, J.R. Hamilton insists that Alexander "bears no responsibility" for either Caranus or his mother Eurydice's death and "is credibly reported to have been distressed by [Olympias's] brutality"[27] when he discovered that the queen had taken advantage of his absence to kill them both. Olympias, Hamilton contends, acted entirely on her own in savagely murdering her former rival and her baby. (According to one particularly lurid contemporary account, Olympias roasted the mother and child alive over hot coals.) Hamilton concedes that Alexander's reputed distress over his stepmother's and half-brother's murders did not stop him from going on to liquidate many of Eurydice's aristocratic male relatives. Still, Hamilton maintains, by eliminating the slain queen's powerful kinsmen, Alexander was merely acting in accordance with a longstanding Macedonian tradition. In Macedon assassination was a time-honored method of safeguarding the throne and as barbaric as the conqueror's behavior may appear by modern standards, at least "Alexander does not seem to have indulged in wanton slaughter."[28]

Alexander Marches South and Has an Encounter with the Oracle at Delphi

Having consolidated his power within Macedon, by the fall of 336 B.C. Alexander was ready to focus his attention on the rest of the vast empire his father had created. Macedon's neighbors had responded to news of their overlord's assassination with unrest verging on out-and-out rebellion. The situation was particularly grave in the Greek states to Macedon's south. Jubilant Athenians offered up prayers of thanksgiving to the gods for the king's death and consecrated a golden wreath in commemoration of his murderer. In Thebes, meanwhile, local officials threatened to expel the Macedonian garrison (occupation troops) Philip had stationed there after the Battle of Chaeronea. With Philip out of the picture and his young and inexperienced son in charge of Macedon, many Greeks believed that the time was ripe to avenge the humiliation they experienced in Chaeronea and regain their independence.

Fearful that Macedon's army would be stretched beyond its limits, the new king's advisers urged caution, admonishing Alexander to forget about the mutinous city-states—at least for the time being—and concentrate on securing the kingdom's borders in the north. But Alexander ignored his counselors' warnings. As usual, he was determined to go his own way. First, he would reassert Macedonian authority in Greece, the young ruler proclaimed. Once that had been accomplished, he would subdue the Thracians, Illyrians, and other rebellious tribes on Macedon's northern frontiers. He intended to show the world that he was as mighty a warrior-king as his father had been.

In the early autumn of 336 B.C. Alexander began his trek southward. He encountered his first challenge near

Alexander, Heracles, and the Oracle at Delphi

As John Maxwell O'Brien notes in his book Alexander the Great: The Invisible Enemy, *Alexander's disrespectful behavior toward the priestess at Delphi was uncharacteristic. " It was uncommon for Alexander to violate a sacred tradition," writes O'Brien. "If anything, he was punctilious [very careful] in observing religious protocol." As O'Brien goes on to observe, however, Alexander's actions at Delphi in 336* B.C. *were*

reminiscent of an encounter his mythical ancestor Heracles was once supposed to have had with the Pythia. Apollo was the god of purification, especially concerning homicide, and Heracles is said to have visited the Delphi Oracle seeking a cure for the madness that made him kill. When the oracle refused to

reply to his request, Heracles seized the tripod, the sacred seat of the prophetess, and threatened to establish his own oracle elsewhere. Apollo then rose to the defense of his priestess and struggled violently with his half-brother. Zeus had to separate his brawling sons with a thunderbolt, but Heracles eventually got the advice he was seeking. Members of this family shared an insistence on having things their own way, and Alexander, who thought of himself as a direct descendant of Heracles, was no exception.

The priestess Pythia sits over the sacred flame at Delphi as she delivers a prophecy.

rugged Mount Ossa at the Vale of Tempe, a river gorge that led southward from Thessaly into central Greece. The Thessalian troops guarding the narrow mountain pass were in no hurry to let Alexander and his men through. While the Thessalians negotiated with his emissaries, writes Fox, Alexander "improvised a bold alternative: he ordered steps to be cut in the cliff-face of nearby Mount Ossa and he led his Macedonians over its peaks by the methods of a mountaineer."[29] Once they discovered that the Macedonians had managed to slip past their army and were now positioned behind them, the dumbfounded Thessalian leadership recognized Alexander as their supreme ruler and placed their renowned cavalry at his disposal. Completely taken off-guard by Alexander's speedy march through Thessaly, Athens and the other city-states of central and southern Greece quickly pledged their allegiance to Philip's young successsor as well.

Before returning to Macedon, Alexander wanted to pay a visit to the oracle (priestly soothsayer) of the god Apollo at Delphi in central Greece. Throughout his career, Alexander would attach enormous importance to divine support and approval. Thus, he was not about to allow an opportunity to consult with the most celebrated oracle in all of Greece pass him by. According to ancient tradition, the Delphic oracle was a woman, a priestess known as the Pythia. After going into a sort of fit or trance (possibly after inhaling a narcotic vapor), the Pythia would deliver prophecies alleged to be straight from Apollo himself. Unfortunately, Alexander arrived at Delphi in early winter, a time of year when the Pythia was strictly forbidden to give prophecies. Never one to take no for an answer, Alexander hunted down the priestess and started dragging her toward the shrine. "Whereupon, apparently overcome by Alexander's forcefulness," reports Plutarch, the Pythia blurted out, "'You are invincible, my son!'"[30] Alexander immediately let go of the struggling woman, declaring that he had heard all he wanted to know. Alexander was obviously flattered by the Pythia's description of him: The only other man in ancient Greek history to be deemed "invincible" by an oracle was the legendary hero Heracles, who was supposedly Alexander's ancestor through his father's line.

Alexander Gets Tough

With Greece again under Macedonian control, Alexander was determined to subjugate once and for all the hostile tribes that continued to threaten his empire's northern and western frontiers. Marching northeastward from Macedon in the spring of 335 B.C., Alexander and his army routed a large Thracian force at Haemus in the Balkan mountain range, slaughtering some fifteen hundred enemy troops in the process. Pushing north toward the Ister (modern Danube) River, he attacked the rebellious Triballian tribe of modern-day Bulgaria, again inflicting huge casualties on his opponents. Ordering his troops to fashion their animal-skin tents into makeshift rafts by filling them with hay, Alexander and five thousand of his troops then crossed the Ister under cover of darkness. At dawn, his forces vanquished the large army of the Getae tribe, which had assembled on the other side of the Ister, thus securing the vast river as Macedon's new northern frontier. Finally turning westward toward modern Albania, Alexander relied on his more sophisticated tactics and weaponry to defeat the tribal warriors of Illyria. The "terrible massacre" that followed his victory "put an end to Illyrian ambition once and for all."[31]

Nevertheless, Alexander was to pay a steep price for the months he had devoted to subduing the Thracians, Illyrians, and other uncooperative tribes who lived on Macedon's remote western and northern frontiers. His campaigning during the spring and summer of 335 B.C. had provided the disgruntled Greek city-states with an unexpected opportunity to rebuild

Alexander and the Macedonian phalanx defeat the Thracians at Mount Haemus in 335 B.C. This victory was one of several Alexander achieved as he marched northeast from Macedon.

Alexander Vanquishes the Thracians at Mount Haemus

"One of the qualities which most clearly distinguishes Alexander from the common run of competent field-commanders is his almost uncanny ability to divine enemy tactics in advance," observes Peter Green in *Alexander of Macedon.* Perhaps in none of his early battles is this remarkable ability more evident than in Alexander's clash with the Thracians at Mount Haemus in the spring of 335 B.C. Alexander noticed that the Thracians had lined up a large number of wagons at the summit of the mountain. Suddenly, the idea occurred to him that the Thracians might not intend the wagons as a defense. Perhaps they were planning to roll the heavy carts downhill into his tightly packed ranks.

Alan Fildes and Joann Fletcher describe what happened next in their biography of the conqueror, *Alexander the Great: Son of the Gods:* "Alexander ordered the heavy infantry to open their ranks to allow the wagons through. Soldiers in the narrower parts of the terrain were told to lie down and interlock their shields over them in 'tortoise' formation. As predicted, the wagons were unleashed, but without the element of surprise they failed to achieve their desired effect." Alexander's scheme had worked perfectly; not one of his soldiers was lost and the unnerved Thracian troops soon fled, leaving behind some fifteen hundred dead and an immense quantity of loot.

their resistance to Macedonian rule. When rumors spread through the peninsula that Alexander had been killed battling the Triballians, Thebes, spurred on by the false report, openly revolted. Determined to keep the empire he had inherited from his father intact, Alexander rushed his exhausted army south from Illyria to Thebes, covering nearly 250 miles in just thirteen days.

Although shocked to discover that Alexander was still alive, the Theban rebels stubbornly refused his demands for their surrender. Peering down on Alexander's assembled forces from a high overlook, the rebels boldly proclaimed that "anyone who wished to join . . . Thebes in freeing the Greeks and destroying the great tyrant of Greece should come over to them."[32] It was at this point, writes Diodorus, that Alexander "decided to destroy the city utterly and by this act of terror take the heart out of anyone else who might venture to rise against him."[33] In the fierce battle that ensued, Alexander's troops indiscriminately massacred Thebes's inhabitants, young and old, male and female alike. "They burst into houses and killed the occupants; others they cut down as they attempted to show fight; others again, even as they clung to temple altars, sparing neither women nor children,"[34] reports the second-century A.D. Greek historian Arrian. By nightfall, some six thousand Thebans lay dead and as many as thirty thousand had been taken prisoner.

To assist him in deciding Thebes's fate, Alexander summoned a meeting of the Panhellenic League of Corinth founded by his father after the Battle of Chaeronea. It is likely that the league's demoralized members did not argue with Alexander's proposals. In the end, the entire city was burned to the ground, with the exception of its temples and the onetime home of the celebrated fifth-century B.C. poet Pindar. Presumably, Pindar's house was preserved because he had penned several poems in honor of Alexander's Macedonian forebears. Almost all of the surviving Thebans were sold as slaves; Alexander spared only the city's priests and priestesses, Pindar's direct descendants, and a small number of nobles who had opposed the rebellion. Confident that his tactics in Thebes had effectively destroyed resistance to his rule throughout the Greek peninsula, writes A.B. Bosworth, "Alexander could justly congratulate himself on a brilliantly successful year. He had reinforced Macedonian control in all directions and given several object lessons illustrating the futility of challenging his awesome military machine."[35] Alexander was now ready to turn his attention to an ambitious new undertaking: conquering the mighty Persian Empire.

Chapter Three

Taking on the Persian Empire

From the beginning of his reign, Alexander had set his sights on invading the Persian Empire. Taking on the Persians, the rulers of the largest kingdom the world had ever seen, had been Philip's last and boldest scheme. By late 335 B.C., having crushed all challenges to his authority in Greece and the Balkans, Alexander was ready to devote himself to the great campaign that had been his father's dream and was to become the central theme of his own military career.

Persia, Greece, and Macedon

The Persians were the ancient inhabitants of what is today southern Iran. During the last half of the sixth century B.C., the Persian kings Cyrus the Great and Cambyses carved out a vast empire in western and central Asia.

Encompassing many different peoples and cultures, the kingdom they built extended from Egypt and Asia Minor (modern Turkey) all the way east to present-day Afghanistan and Pakistan. On the coast of Asia Minor, the Persian, or Achaemenid, Empire, as it was also known, included a number of former Greek colonies, most notably the wealthy trading centers of Ephesus, Miletus, and Priene.

In 490 B.C. Cambyses' successor, Darius I, launched an unsuccessful military campaign to extend Persian control across the Aegean Sea and into Greece itself. A decade later, the Persians were back under their new king, Xerxes I. Once again the allied Greek forces defeated their Asian invaders, but not before Persian troops had sacked Athens. For the Greeks, the Persian army's

The Great Persian Empire

Although the Greeks and Macedonians tended to look down on the Persians as less civilized than themselves, the "Persians were a highly sophisticated people," note Alan Fildes and Joann Fletcher in *Alexander the Great: Son of the Gods*. In 334 B.C. the Achaemenid Empire had already been in existence for more than two hundred years and "was a source of enormous wealth—the Persian monarch was the richest man on earth," write the two historians. From the unrivaled splendor of his main palace at Persepolis, the "Great King" of Persia, the "Chosen One" of the chief Persian god Ahura Mazda, reigned over a huge and diverse population, including Babylonians, Arabs, Egyptians, Indians, and Greeks, among others, and a territory that encompassed some 1 million square miles.

Despite the enormous size of his empire, the Great King was able to communicate quickly with even the most distant corners of his realm by means of an efficient network of highways, broad roads that also fed the empire's prudently managed finances by serving as vital continental trade routes. From the western coast of Asia Minor, notes Pierre Briant in *Alexander the Great*, the most celebrated of these highways, the Royal Road, "ran through Ancyra (present-day Ankara), . . . Babylonia, and Susia. 'Everywhere along it,' an ancient writer reported, 'are royal staging-posts and excellent hostels.'" The Persian Empire's most important cities—Persepolis, Susa, and Babylon—"were linked to India and Egypt by other royal highways, traveled by the king's armies and couriers under the watchful protection of highway sentinels," writes Briant.

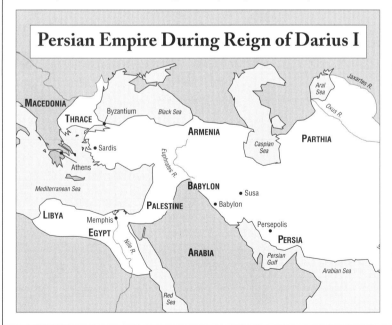

Persian Empire During Reign of Darius I

desecration and torching of Athens's holiest shrines in 480 B.C. was never forgotten: Even after nearly a century and a half, the invaders' sacrilegious looting of the temples of the Acropolis and the city's other hallowed sanctuaries still bothered the Greeks.

Shortly after his victory over the allied Greek forces at Chaeronea in 338 B.C., Philip announced his intention to invade the Persian Empire on Greece's behalf at a meeting of the League of Corinth. Revenge for Xerxes' attack on Greece 140 years earlier and the liberation of the former Greek colonies in western Asia Minor were Philip's official reasons for the expedition. In truth, asserts scholar Ian Worthington, the Macedonian king's chief motive for his well-publicized crusade against Persia was probably "to win goodwill in the Greek world."[36] Although he had gained control of the Greek peninsula by force of arms, Philip still hoped that its inhabitants would someday come to accept him as their legitimate ruler. That Philip shared his southern neighbors' hatred for their ancestral enemy and was even prepared to spearhead a military campaign against the Persians would help cement Macedon's claim to lead the Greeks after the Battle of Chaeronea. By the summer of 336, the king's plan for a punitive expedition against the Achaemenid Empire was beginning to fall into place. Just weeks before his assassination, Philip sent an advance force of some ten thousand

Macedonians across the Hellespont (modern Dardanelles), the narrow waterway that divides the European continent from Asia Minor, to prepare the way for his main army.

One of Alexander's first actions after assuming the throne later that summer was to reassert his kingdom's commitment to the Persian expedition. A year and a half later, after quelling the revolt at Thebes, Alexander was finally ready to focus his full attention on the ambitious scheme he had inherited from his father. Although his top military advisers strongly urged putting off the invasion until the new monarch could find a suitable wife and provide heirs to the throne, Alexander refused to listen. The young king "may simply have been impatient to conduct a major campaign—for his desire for glory is undoubted—but it is not impossible that he was thinking of the state of the Macedonian economy,"[37] observes J.R. Hamilton. Philip's endless military campaigning and lavish spending habits had left Macedon's economy on the brink of bankruptcy. Adding to Alexander's financial woes were his own costly military operations in the Balkans and Greece. The Persian Empire, in contrast, was famously wealthy, and any nation that managed to conquer it could expect abundant riches. Thus, Alexander's determination to invade Asia immediately may have had almost as much to do with his kingdom's financial trou-

The Macedonian phalanx was a meticulously drilled infantry unit comprised of peasants who wielded long, iron-tipped pikes with deadly precision.

bles as it did with his deep craving for personal fame and glory.

Alexander's Invasion Force

Alexander spent the winter of 335–334 preparing for his new expedition, which was slated to begin in the spring. It was decided that the veteran general Antipater should remain behind with a force of fourteen thousand to keep the peace in Alexander's vast European domain, while another of Philip's trusted generals, Parmenion, would act as Alexander's second-in-command for the Asian campaign.

The force that Alexander assembled for his upcoming expedition was one of the greatest armies in the ancient world. Although pride of place was given to the companion cavalry, whose nearly two thousand horsemen came from the Macedonian aristocracy, the army's backbone was its large infantry phalanx. Recruited almost exclusively from Macedon's peasantry, these meticulously drilled, *sarissa*-wielding foot soldiers had formed the heart of Philip's formidable military machine as well. Smaller specialist units, including javelin throwers, archers, and light infantry, were also part of Alexander's invasion force. Illyrians, Thracians, and other Balkan peoples were well represented in these units; some eight thousand troops from the Balkan region are believed to have crossed into Asia with Alexander along with at least twenty thousand Macedonians.

Alexander also recruited troops for his expedition from the city-states of the League of Corinth, the pan-Greek coalition that Philip had founded and the new king now headed. In total, about seventy-five hundred troops were sent by the states of central and southern Greece to assist in Alexander's Persian crusade. Although the number of Greek soldiers in the invasion force was relatively small, Alexander placed a high value on their participation in his campaign. For one thing, Greek representation in the expedition lent credence to Alexander's claim that his invasion of Asia was motivated not by greed or personal ambition but by a noble desire to avenge the humiliations inflicted by the Persians on the Greek people. For another, Alexander seems to have envisioned the troops as a sort of insurance against any future Greek rebellions like the one he had just crushed in Thebes. In effect, writes historian Pierre Briant, the "Greek soldiers would serve as hostages to ensure their cities' loyalty"[38] while Alexander and a large portion of the Macedonian army were in Asia.

To accompany his multinational fighting force to Asia, Alexander drafted hundreds of specialists and technicians. There were engineers to design siege machines, roads, and bridges; architects to oversee the building of new cities; and surveyors to gather information about potential campsites and routes. He also included a remarkable number and variety of scholars in his expeditionary team. Undoubtedly

Alexander Takes a Detour to Troy

After arriving in Illium—the ancient site of Troy—Alexander's first act was to offer a lavish sacrifice at the supposed tomb of the legendary Greek champion of the Trojan War, Achilles. Hephaestion, the king's best friend since childhood, also paid tribute to the tomb of Patroclus—Achilles' closest companion in Homer's *Iliad* and *Odyssey*. At the temple of Athena, Alexander solemnly dedicated his own armor to the goddess, who was the patron of not only wisdom and cities but also the disciplined aspects of war, such as strategy and training. In return, Athena's priests presented Alexander with a shield and armor said to date from the era of Achilles. Alexander, always eager to associate himself with his hero and supposed ancestor, was thrilled with the priests' gift. According to Robin Lane Fox in *Alexander the Great*, "No gesture could speak more clearly for his personal ideals. Homer's Achilles, too, had received divine armor of his own before going out to battle.... Alexander had now equaled his hero, and such was his favor for the Trojan shield and armor that they would accompany him to war as far as India and back, carried before him by his bodyguard-at-arms."

reflecting the influence of his boyhood tutor Aristotle, Alexander recruited botanists, zoologists, geologists, and a host of other naturalists for his campaign. Over the years, they would collect thousands of plant, animal, and mineral specimens, most of which were sent back to the great centers of scientific learning in Greece. Among the other scholars who took part in the expedition were poets and philosophers to entertain and enlighten the king, and a historian—Aristotle's nephew Callisthenes—to serve as the campaign's official chronicler and propagandist, for Alexander always took great care with his public image. Callisthenes' main task was to favorably portray the king's exploits in order to impress his subjects in Macedon and throughout the Greek-speaking world.

The Battle at the Granicus River

Early in the spring of 334 B.C., Alexander led the large and diverse expeditionary team that he had been assembling for the past several months out of Macedon and toward the Hellespont. Immediately after crossing the Hellespont into modern-day Turkey, the king left his army to make a brief pilgrimage to the coastal city of Illium, the site of ancient Troy. At Troy, Alexander offered sacrifices to the Greek war goddess, Athena, and visited the tomb of his hero and alleged ancestor, Achilles. Rejoining his army at the

nearby town of Arisbe, Alexander commanded his troops to march east.

A few days later at the Granicus (modern Koçabas) River, Alexander came upon Persian troops for the first time since crossing into Asia. A large Persian army, nearly equal in size to his own, was assembled on the eastern side of the river, at the top of a muddy and steep embankment. The ancient sources disagree as to exactly what happened next, but in his lengthy account of the encounter at Granicus, Arrian contends that Alexander, brushing aside Parmenion's advice to delay attack, boldly led his troops across the rain-swollen river and up the slippery embankment to where the enemy was gathered. In the hand-to-hand battle that ensued, reports Arrian, "Persian lances flew thick and fast, the long Macedonian spears thrust and stabbed." Alexander, "an unmistakable figure in magnificent armor," was "in the thick of it, charging at the head of his men straight for the spot where the Persian commanders stood."[39] According to Diodorus, the Persians, intent on disposing of their enemy's commander in chief as quickly as possible, "braved every imaginable danger in their attempts to slay him." Alexander's "breastplate was struck twice, his helmet once, and three strokes fell on [his] shield,"[40] yet the young king never wavered, fighting with a courage and resolve worthy of his hero Achilles.

Alexander and his cavalry cross the Granicus River in modern-day Turkey to engage the Persian army for the first time since crossing into Asia.

In the end, the allied forces' superior tactics, discipline, and weaponry won the day. According to Arrian, Alexander lost perhaps a hundred men in the fighting while Persian casualties numbered well into the thousands. "The death toll would have been even greater," note Alan Fildes and Joann Fletcher, "had the Macedonians been ordered to pursue the fleeing enemy."[41] Instead, Alexander focused his efforts on the five to six thousand Greek mercenaries serving with the Persian army. Although they pleaded for their lives, Alexander showed no mercy toward the Persian king's Greek hirelings, whom he considered contemptible traitors. "Ordering a combined assault by infantry and cavalry," Arrian writes, "Alexander quickly had them surrounded and butchered to a man."[42]

Alexander was far more compassionate and generous in his treatment of his own troops. "For the wounded he showed deep concern," reports Arrian. "He visited them all and examined their wounds, asking each man how and in what circumstances his wound was received, and allowing him to tell his story and exaggerate as much as he pleased."[43] For his fallen soldiers, Alexander arranged magnificent burials. He also granted their family members lifetime exemptions from military service and property taxes. According to Diodorus, Alexander figured that these honors and privileges would "create in his men greater enthusiasm to face the hazards of battle."[44] The "ulterior pragmatic motive," notes Peter Green, "is seldom far to seek in [Alexander's] actions."[45]

"Liberating" Asia Minor

News of Alexander's triumph at Granicus traveled quickly through western Asia Minor. At the strategic stronghold of Sardis in the province of Lydia, the Persian satrap, or governor, surrendered before Alexander's army even reached the city's walls. Turning back toward the Aegean Sea, Alexander next swept down the coast of Asia Minor, where most of the Greek-speaking cities scurried to open their gates to his forces. "Whether they acted out of fear or

respect is unknown," notes scholar Rick Black, "but the inhabitants greeted him as a liberator and handed him their treasury."[46] Ephesus, Priene, and Magnesia were officially freed from their Persian overlords, and in stark contrast to his policies in mainland Greece, where he had imposed pro-Macedonian oligarchies (a type of government in which power is held by a few), Alexander ordered the Greek cities of Asia Minor to form democracies. According to J.R. Hamilton, these orders did not indicate a newfound "preference on Alexander's part for democracy . . . but, since Persia had maintained oligarchies in Asia Minor, Alexander was bound to take the opposite line."[47] In reality, the supposedly liberated democracies of western Asia Minor remained firmly under Alexander's control. The old Persian tribute (enforced payment) was abolished, notes Stoneman, but the "cities promised henceforth to pay 'contributions' to their new leader. Some subtler minds may have been able to make the distinction between this and tribute."[48]

Although Alexander clearly interpreted the term *liberation* in a very restricted sense, he did not encounter any serious resistance along the western coast of Asia Minor until he reached the port of Miletus. At Miletus, Persian defenders assisted by several hundred Greek mercenaries put up a brave fight, but proved no match for Alexander's state-of-the-art siege equipment including massive stone-throwing catapults and 180-feet-high seige towers with draw bridges. About three hundred of the Greek hirelings fled to a nearby island, where they undoubtedly expected to be slaughtered by Alexander's troops, just as their fellow mercenaries had been after the Battle of Granicus. This time around, however, Alexander took a different tack. When he saw that the fugitives were prepared to "fight to the death," writes Arrian, "he was moved to pity by their courage and loyalty" and pledged to spare them "on condition of their serving in future under his own command."[49] The "fact was that Alexander saw that his policy of treating

such men as traitors was mistaken," contends Hamilton, "and, ready as always to learn by his mistakes, decided to enroll in his army 300 valuable recruits."[50]

After taking Miletus, Alexander continued his march southward, heading for the heavily fortified city of Halicarnassus in the province of Caria. Following a lengthy siege, Alexander secured control of the Persian stronghold. Then he restored Ada, the ousted queen of Caria and his avid supporter, to her throne. In gratitude, Ada adopted the young king as her son and heir. This was a major coup for Alexander, notes O'Brien, since his adoption by the Carian queen "would make it possible

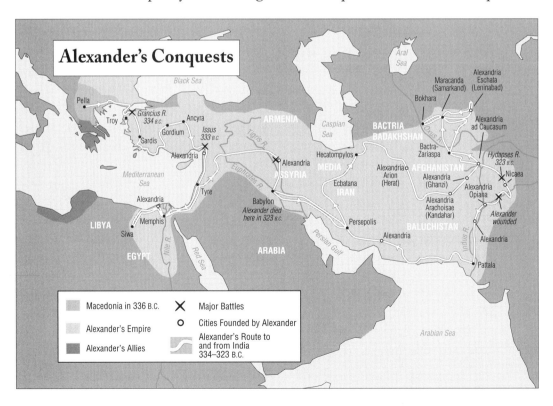

Alexander's Conquests

for Alexander to assume the throne without opposition when Ada died. It was typical of his masterful diplomacy."[51]

Untying the Gordian Knot

Leaving Caria, Alexander resumed his march along the southern edge of Asia Minor, establishing control over the coast as far as Lycia. Then he veered northward toward the region of Phrygia in central Asia Minor, where he planned to spend the winter at the ancient city of Gordium.

At Gordium, Alexander heard about an old tradition involving a wagon that had supposedly belonged to Gordius, the founder of Phrygia. The wagon's yoke was fastened to a pole by a knot so complex that it was impossible to determine where the knot began and ended. It was prophesied that whoever managed to unravel the knot would rule all of Asia. Over the years, countless men had attempted to untie it, but not one had succeeded. This challenge proved irresistible to Alexander. The king demanded to be taken to the ancient palace where the wagon was kept. Yet no matter how hard Alexander pulled, the knot refused to loosen. "Alexander contemplated the problem for a while," writes Richard Stoneman, "and then with his usual impetuous disregard for little difficulties, he cut through the knot with his sword."[52]

Alexander, who always placed great importance on oracles and heavenly signs, was eager for confirmation that

Alexander uses his sword to cut through the Gordian knot after he was unable to loosen it by hand.

he had indeed passed the test of the Gordian knot and fulfilled the ancient prophecy. "That very night," reports Arrian, "there was lightning and thunder."[53] Alexander and his soothsayers took this as a signal of approval from the supreme god, Zeus, who was often depicted hurling a thunderbolt. The next day Alexander offered a sacrifice in thanksgiving to Zeus for sending an unmistakable sign that he had solved the Gordian knot and was destined to rule over all Asia.

The Battle of Issus

Alexander's exact intentions regarding the Persian Empire when he landed on the Turkish coast in the spring of 334 B.C. are unknown. Did he really mean to stop at freeing the Greek cities of Asia Minor from Persian rule, or even then, did he dream of conquering all of Asia to the farthest reaches of the Achaemenid domain? That question will remain forever unanswerable, but it is clear that by

Alexander's Commanders

When Alexander launched his invasion of the Persian Empire, his top generals included many veteran warriors such as his second in command, Parmenion, who had faithfully served his father for decades, and the elderly Antigonus Monophthalmus, better known as "Antigonus the One-Eyed." In time, however, Alexander would come to rely more and more on noblemen of his own age, most notably Hephaestion, his closest friend since childhood. Among Alexander's other youthful commanders were Craterus, Ptolemy, and Seleucus, all of whom were assigned to lead battalions and regiments of foot soldiers or horsemen. In 330 B.C., Alexander ordered the murder of the aging Parmenion, whom he deemed as a security risk after his son Philotas, a cavalry commander, was found guilty of failing to report an assassination plot against the king. As his new second in command, Alexander appointed his friend Craterus, widely considered the conqueror's most talented young general. But in every instance throughout the king's long Persian campaign, notes Pierre Briant in *Alexander the Great*, "the final decisions were made by Alexander, who fought in person at the head of his troops astride his warhorse Bucephalas."

One seasoned Macedonian commander who had no role in Alexander's Asian crusade was Attalus, the man whose insulting remarks at Philip and his niece Eurydice's wedding banquet had so infuriated the nineteen-year-old prince. Shortly after assuming the throne, Alexander ordered Attalus's arrest for carrying on what the king considered a treasonous correspondence with the Athenian orator Demosthenes, one of Macedon's most ardent Greek critics. Philip's old general and kinsman by marriage was killed by the man whom Alexander had sent to apprehend him while Attalus was allegedly resisting arrest.

The Persian king Darius and his army retreat from Alexander's men outside the village of Issus in 333 B.C. Darius managed to escape with his life.

the time Alexander departed Gordium a year later, his ambitions had expanded well beyond recovering the traditionally Greek territories of Asia Minor. Alexander and his army were bound for Asia Minor's Mediterranean coast to conquer lands that had never been Greek and, even more significantly, to hunt down—and defeat in battle—the supreme ruler of the Persian Empire himself, the "Great King," Darius III.

In the meantime, concerned by reports of Alexander's victories, Darius had been busy assembling a large army at Babylon (in present-day Iraq). According to some ancient sources, the Great King marshaled over 300,000 troops in an

effort to stop the Macedonian conqueror in his tracks. The fateful meeting between Darius's huge force and Alexander's much smaller but battle-hardened army finally arrived in the autumn of 333 B.C. near the border of modern-day Turkey and Syria.

Darius's forces took up position on a narrow plain between the Amanus Mountains and the Mediterranean, just outside the village of Issus. Because the narrowness of the plain made it difficult for the much larger Persian force to outmaneuver Alexander's army, it would prove a poor choice of battlefield on Darius's part. As the two forces faced each other across the Pinarus

River, Alexander sent for his officers and, Arrian reports, "appealed to them for confidence and courage in the coming fight. 'Remember,' he said, 'that already danger has often threatened you and you have looked it triumphantly in the face.'"[54] In an impressive display of personal courage, the king, plunging into the river astride his warhorse Bucephalas, led his cavalry in a frontal assault against the huge Persian army assembled on the opposite bank. "Alexander turned his gaze in all directions, seeking Darius," writes Diodorus. "As soon as he saw him, he raced into the field with his horsemen, straight for the Great King in person."[55] Darius, terrified of falling into his enemy's hands, seized the reins of his war chariot and fled the battlefield. Soon the entire Persian army was in retreat.

Alexander pursued Darius eastward for many miles, but the Persian king had a considerable head start. When darkness fell, Alexander gave up the chase and returned to Issus. Entering Darius's deserted tent, he was delighted to find elaborately carved gold caskets, costly furniture, and thousands of talents (large monetary units representing a certain amount of silver, usually about fifty-eight pounds). In a nearby tent, Alexander discovered Darius's frightened mother, daughters, and wife, along with a few female Persian attendants. Alexander chivalrously assured his female hostages that he "wished them to retain all the marks, ceremonies, and titles of royalty, as he had not fought Darius with any personal bitterness, but had made legitimate war for the sovereignty of Asia,"[56] writes Arrian. Because they would give him "a decided advantage in future negotiations" with Darius, notes John Maxwell O'Brien, to Alexander, "these women were . . . priceless political commodities." Nevertheless, O'Brien contends, "one should not dismiss the genuine pity and compassion on Alexander's part in this episode, or underestimate the impact of his magnanimity and charm. The royal women were said to have praised him as the one man to whom it was right to lose an empire."[57]

Darius's vast empire was not yet lost, however. "Issus was a great victory, but by no means a decisive one," writes one historian. "So long as Darius himself remained at large, there was no question of the war being over."[58]

Chapter Four

"The King of All Asia"

Shortly after his defeat at Issus, Darius sent a message to Alexander offering friendship and pleading for the release of his wife and other female relatives. Alexander contemptuously rebuffed the king's peace overtures, reminding him of his ancestor Xerxes' unprovoked assault on Greece's holiest shrines and demanding Darius's immediate and unconditional surrender. "In future," Alexander wrote haughtily, "let any communication you wish to make with me be addressed to the King of All Asia." If "you wish to dispute this title," he admonished Darius, "stand and fight for it and do not run away. Wherever you hide yourself, be sure I shall seek you out."[59] Despite his threat to seek Darius out, however, in his quest to rule "All Asia" (that is, the Persian Empire), Alexander had other, even more pressing business to attend to first. Before marching eastward in pursuit of his rival, Alexander was determined to secure control of Asia's strategically vital Mediterranean coastline as well as the vast and wealthy North African kingdom of Egypt.

Alexander's Bloody Mediterranean Campaign

In late 333 B.C. Alexander departed Issus for southwestern Asia's Mediterranean coast and its great Phoenician seaports. Corresponding roughly to the coastal regions of modern Syria, Lebanon, and Israel, Phoenicia was an ancient nation whose seafaring inhabitants established trading cities throughout the Mediterranean basin. Alexander, who lacked a strong navy of his own, was determined to overcome his enemy's superiority at sea by isolating Darius's large fleet of warships from its vital Mediterranean bases: the bustling Phoenician seaports that supplied the Persian navy with freshwater and food. Stunned by Alexander's triumph over the huge Achaemenid army at Issus, one Phoenician city after another surrendered to the Macedonians without a fight, including the critical trading and naval centers of Sidon and Byblos.

Alexander's triumphant march down the Mediterranean coast came to an abrupt halt just south of Sidon at Tyre. Hoping to remain neutral in the struggle between Alexander and Darius, the people of Tyre refused Alexander's request to enter their city, declaring that "Tyre would admit neither Persians nor

Siege of Tyre

North or Sidonian port

Old city of Tyre

Alexander's mole

New city of Tyre

South or Egyptian port

Macedonians while hostilities between the two continued,"[60] writes John Maxwell O'Brien. Despite Alexander's impressive reputation as a fighter, the Tyrians were not intimidated by the Macedonian leader. Tyre's location about a half-mile off the mainland in deep, windswept waters and its 150-foot-high stone walls had convinced its citizens that their city was unconquerable. As it turned out, however, the Tyrians had underestimated both Alexander's remarkable ingenuity and his ironclad resolve.

Alexander launched his siege of Tyre in January 332 B.C., writes Diodorus, "determined to run every risk and make every effort to save the Macedonian army from being held in contempt by a single undistinguished city."[61] Alexander devised an imaginative scheme to take the seemingly impregnable island-city: He would fashion a causeway to span the divide between Tyre and the coast. Constructing the stone and wood causeway was a time-consuming project, and as the work slowly progressed, the Tyrians did everything they could think of to harass the causeway's builders, from shooting flaming arrows at them to showering them with red-hot sand. In August 332, more than six months after the siege had begun, reinforced by warships from Sidon and Macedon's other newfound Phoenician allies,

Alexander's troops finally managed to break through the Tyrian defenses. Determined to send a message to the city's neighbors in Phoenicia, Alexander made the people of Tyre pay a terrible price for their defiance. Eight thousand Tyrian soldiers and civilians were slaughtered during Alexander's sack of the city. After the fighting was over, two thousand men of military age were rounded up and crucified along the seashore, "a grim warning of the futility of resisting the conqueror,"[62] notes A.B. Bosworth. Alexander then ordered the enslavement of Tyre's remaining inhabitants—some thirty thousand men, women, and children.

Leaving the smoking ruins of Tyre behind, Alexander continued his relentless march through the great naval and commercial centers of the Mediterranean's southeastern lip. Not until he reached the heavily fortified city of Gaza did he again encounter opposition. Because Gaza was situated on a high mound encircled by deep sand, the Persian commander of the city's garrison, Batis, was convinced that it could withstand any assault. While Alexander's army was still bogged down in Tyre, Batis had prepared for a long siege by hiring Arab mercenaries and laying in several months' worth of provisions. Yet even though transporting his massive siege towers through the fine, shifting sand that surrounded Gaza proved more time-consuming and arduous than he

In 332 B.C. Alexander lays siege to Tyre after the Tyrians refused to admit the conqueror into the city.

had expected and Batis's mercenaries launched continual raids on his lines, Alexander was undeterred. Even after sustaining two serious wounds, one in his shoulder and one in his leg, Alexander's deep-seated aversion to failure drove him on.

When rebellious Gaza finally fell after a grueling two-month siege, as in Tyre, Alexander's revenge was savage. The city's ten thousand defenders were systematically slaughtered and their families sold into slavery. For the garrison commander, Batis, who remained silent when brought before the Macedonian king, Alexander reserved an unusually cruel punishment. Infuriated by his opponent's stubborn refusal to acknowledge his triumph, Alexander ordered that Batis's feet be pierced and leather thongs inserted through the holes. The thongs were then attached to the back of the king's chariot, and the hapless commander was dragged around the city walls until he was dead. Although some ancient sources, including Arrian's generally admiring biography of Alexander, leave out this gruesome episode, many modern historians believe it to be genuine. Writes British scholar Bosworth:

> The story cannot be proved false, certainly not on the basis of its omission by Arrian, and there was every reason why Alexander, irked by the long delays at Tyre and Gaza, should have wished to give a terrible object lesson to any community or commander who

Alexander visits the oracle at the temple of the Egyptian god Amun, where he learned it was Amun's will that he was destined to conquer the entire world.

Alexander's Harrowing Journey Through the Desert to Siwa

Callisthenes, the official chronicler of the Persian expedition, wrote a very dramatic history of the king's trek through the Western Desert to the oracle at Siwa that would later serve as Plutarch's primary source for his version of the journey. "As befits a work of propaganda," writes Michael Wood in his *In the Footsteps of Alexander the Great*, "Callisthenes's account stressed providential happenings." Callisthenes, clearly anxious to demonstrate that the gods were on his master's side, filled his description of Alexander's pilgrimage to the sanctuary of Zeus-Amun with "romantic embellishments, omens and signs, all of which would suggest to the reader divine intervention," notes Wood.

Although Alexander and his companions actually followed a well-traveled caravan route through the desert to Siwa, if Callisthenes is to be believed, they confronted one life-threatening peril after another during the course of their trip. Just four days after entering the desert, the group managed to run out of water and would have perished if not for the sudden violent downpour that occurred, a gift sent directly from Zeus himself, according to Callisthenes. Later, a terrible sandstorm obliterated all the desert landmarks, causing the small party to lose their way. Suddenly two crows miraculously appeared and guided the frightened group to the safety of a nearby oasis. Once again, suggests Callisthenes, the gods must have been looking out for the Macedonian king.

might have the temerity to resist his progress. The fact that the episode is singularly revolting is not argument against its historicity [historical authenticity].[63]

Alexander in Egypt

With the entire length of Asia's Mediterranean coastline now under his control, Alexander focused his attention on the ancient North African kingdom of Egypt. He went to Egypt prepared to fight, but when he arrived at the border town of Pelusium in late 332 B.C., Alexander found himself being welcomed as a savior and deliverer. Once one of the greatest powers in the world, Egypt had been an extremely reluctant vassal of the Achaemenid rulers. More than anything else, the Egyptians resented the Persians' contemptuous disregard for their kingdom's ancient religious traditions. Alexander, a profoundly devout man who never had any problem worshipping foreign deities similar to his own gods, rapidly won the trust of

The Famed City of Alexandria

According to one ancient account, when Alexander the Great was formulating his plans for Alexandria, he scattered barley meal (a type of flour) on the ground to show where he wanted the city walls and the main streets to be placed. Suddenly, a large flock of birds of all sizes and kinds swooped down on the grain, devouring every bit of it. The ever-superstitious Alexander was dismayed, interpreting the incident as a bad omen for his new project. Eager to please his master, the king's soothsayer, Aristander, immediately reassured Alexander that the birds' eating of the barley meal was actually a good sign. The city would have the most plentiful and beneficial resources, Aristander predicted, and be like a mother to people from many different nations.

As it turned out, Aristander's glowing prediction regarding Alexandria came closer to the truth than the old soothsayer could have imagined. In the decades following Alexander's death, Alexandria would become one of the world's foremost intellectual, cultural, and commercial centers, attracting scholars, merchants, and artists from a host of different lands. Perhaps the most celebrated of the city's many impressive buildings was the Library of Alexandria, which reportedly contained more than 500,000 papyrus scrolls. Alexandria was also renowned for its gigantic lighthouse, the Pharos (named after the small island on which it was built). Standing more than four hundred feet tall, the lighthouse, which was destroyed by a series of earthquakes in the 1400s, was long considered one of the Seven Wonders of the World. Today, more than two thousand years after its founding, Alexandria is still a thriving and cosmopolitan metropolis. Home to more than 3 million people, it is Egypt's second biggest city and leading port.

Alexander (crouching, right) shares his design for the city of Alexandria with his chief architect.

Egypt's influential priesthood by publicly sacrificing to their deities and promising to restore their country's long-neglected temples and other shrines. So grateful were the Egyptian clergy for delivering them from their oppressors that they even anointed Alexander as their new pharaoh, or king, in a magnificent ceremony at Memphis, the ancient Egyptian capital. The Persian satrap Mazaces, who possessed only a few troops and had no help from outsiders, had little choice but to bend to the popular will and recognize Alexander as Egypt's rightful ruler. In return, eager to take advantage of Mazaces' experience, Alexander provided the former governor with a post in his new administration, although he cautiously assigned the highest political offices in Egypt to Macedonians, Greeks, and native Egyptians and kept the military firmly under Macedonian control.

As he had done nearly three years earlier in Troy, in Egypt Alexander parted with his main army for a time to embark on a personal pilgrimage. In January 331 B.C. the king and a small group of companions and guides set off on an arduous three-hundred-mile journey across the blazing Western Desert to the oasis of Siwa, home of the famous oracle of the Egyptian god Amun. The Greeks equated Amun with their own supreme god, Zeus, and Alexander, who had always placed great faith in

oracles, was determined to consult with Amun's priestly soothsayer. No one knows precisely what transpired in the inner sanctuary of the temple at Siwa. According to Plutarch's account, Alexander asked the oracle "whether it was god's will that he should rule over the whole world," to which "the god replied that such was his will."[64] Whatever Alexander may have heard at Siwa, write Fildes and Fletcher, he was "sufficiently satisfied" with his visit "to present magnificent offerings to the oracle, and for the rest of his life he sent frequent gifts to its priests, together with more questions."[65]

Around the time of his pilgrimage to Siwa, Alexander commissioned the construction of a city at the mouth of the Nile River that was to become one of his most celebrated and enduring legacies: Alexandria, Egypt. One of the most illustrious cities in human history, Alexandria would soon become a major commercial hub as well as the cultural and intellectual center of the entire Mediterranean world. According to Diodorus, Alexander not only chose the site of the new city but also nearly single-handedly designed its layout. Outlining it in the shape of a Macedonian military cloak, the king instructed his builders where to position the marketplace, the temples, and the outer fortifications. By most accounts, Alexander was as skilled a city planner as he was a soldier.

Alexandria, wrote Diodorus, "was conveniently situated near the harbor of Pharos, and by selecting the right angle of the streets, Alexander made the city breathe with the etesian [westerly] winds so that as they blow across a great expanse of sea, they cool the air of the town, and so he provided its inhabitants with a moderate climate and good health."[66]

A few months after founding Alexandria, Alexander received a second envoy from Darius. This time Darius was prepared to offer Alexander all Persian territory west of the Euphrates River, the hand of his eldest daughter in marriage, and ten thousand talents in exchange for peace and the safe return of his family. Impressed by Darius's generous terms, Parmenion remarked that if he were Alexander, he would accept the king's offer. "So would I," Alexander reportedly fired back, "if I were Parmenion."[67] Nothing less than total conquest would satisfy Alexander, particularly now that he had secured Egypt as well as virtually all of Asia Minor. Darius's offer did not interest him, Alexander wrote haughtily to the Great King, because the entire Persian Empire and its treasures would soon be his anyway; as far as Darius's daughter was concerned, should he decide to wed her, he would do so with or without her father's permission. Back in Babylon, Darius saw no other alternative and began to prepare for all-out war.

The Battle of Gaugamela

Alexander was also preparing for what he hoped would be his final showdown with his Persian rival. Shortly after receiving Darius's second letter, Alexander led his forces out of Egypt and back to Asia Minor. From there, the Macedonian army headed eastward across the Euphrates River, reaching Gaugamela (north of modern Baghdad, Iraq), where Alexander had been informed that the Persian army was waiting, in early autumn 331 B.C.

At Gaugamela, Alexander, whose own forces have been estimated at 47,000, was confronted with a huge enemy force of some 200,000 foot and horse soldiers (one ancient source even claims that Darius mustered 500,000 troops). The Great King's imposing army also included Indian war elephants from the farthest reaches of his vast empire and two hundred scythed chariots. The Roman historian Quintus Curtius Rufus describes these fear-inspiring vehicles: "Iron-pointed spears protruded ahead of the horses; three sword-blades were affixed on either side of the yoke; javelin points stuck outward from the spokes of the wheels; scythe blades welded to the wheel rims mowed down everything the horses encountered in their charge."[68] Resolved to avoid the same mistake he had made at the Battle of Issus, this time Darius chose for his battlefield a wide plain ideally suited for his immense force and particularly his large chariot and cavalry divisions.

The Macedonian and Persian armies engage in battle at Gaugamela in 331 B.C. Alexander's forces dealt Darius and his men a crippling defeat.

Although taken off guard by the size of Darius's army, displaying once again the military genius that many historians consider his greatest gift, Alexander soon devised a daring but brilliant battle plan. According to Caroline Alexander:

> The Macedonians assembled facing Darius, who was dead center in his line of formation, surrounded by bodyguards. On command the Macedonians advanced in perfect order, with Alexander on the right; but instead of moving straight ahead, their line swung out, placing Alexander at the tip of a wedge, facing Darius. Alexander, knowing

that he was utterly outflanked anyway, had decided to lure Darius to his wings, then attack the weakened Persian center. The ploy worked. With both flanks desperately engaged . . . Alexander spotted the anticipated fatal weakening in the enemy line. Charging at the head of his Companion Cavalry, he broke through, cutting Darius off from his second-in-command.[69]

As at Issus two years earlier, Darius turned and ran for his life. Realizing that their leader had abandoned them, Darius's demoralized forces also started to retreat. With his victory assured,

Alexander galloped off the field after the Great King. Although Alexander chased his opponent for seventy-five miles, Darius, accompanied by his cousin and cavalry commander, Bessus, managed to elude his pursuers, eventually making his way to his royal palace at Ecbatana in modern-day Iran. Once again Alexander's hopes of killing or capturing his rival for the Persian throne had been dashed. In the wake of Alexander's decisive victory in Gaugamela, however, Darius's prestige and authority had suffered a catastrophic blow. Writes Peter Green:

The oracle at Gordium had foretold that Alexander would become . . . king of the Persian Empire and Darius' legitimate successor. It was thus, somewhat prematurely, that he had bidden Darius address him [the King of All Asia] when they exchanged letters. After Gaugamela the claim looked a good deal more plausible [convincing].[70]

Babylon and Susa

Although Alexander had every intention of hunting down the man who still

Alexander enters the city of Babylon on a chariot drawn by an ornately decorated elephant. The city's inhabitants welcomed the conqueror as their liberator from the Persians.

called himself the rightful ruler of all Asia, he decided that disposing of Darius could wait until he had claimed the three wealthiest cities of the vast Achaemenid Empire: Babylon, Susa, and Persepolis. Consequently, on October 2, 331 B.C., the day after the battle at Gaugamela, Alexander ordered his army to march southeastward toward the fabled city of Babylon.

At the northern portal of Babylon, the spectacular Ishtar Gate, the Persian satrap Mazaeus surrendered peacefully to Alexander while the city's cheering populace hailed the Macedonian king as their deliverer. Like the Egyptians, the Babylonians had long resented the Persians' obvious disdain for their ancient religious traditions. In keeping with his reputation for respecting local religious practices and beliefs, Alexander made a point of meeting with Babylon's high priests immediately after entering the city. With their direction, he offered sacrifices at the shrine of the chief Babylonian god, Marduk. "By honoring native traditions in this way," write Alan Fildes and Joann Fletcher, "Alexander earned the eternal gratitude of Babylon's priests and people."[71]

In late November Alexander departed Babylon for Susa, another wealthy ancient city that had been conquered many years earlier by Darius's Achaemenid predecessors. Like Babylon, Susa surrendered to Alexander without a fight. Located near the border of modern Iran and Iraq at the head of the Persian Gulf, Susa was the Achaemenids' winter capital. At the sumptuous royal palace, Alexander sat on Darius's golden throne and was thrilled to discover Greek artwork that had been taken by the Persians from the sack of Athens a century and a half earlier. Alexander also found fifty thousand gold talents and great quantities of gold and silver jewelry and ornaments in the palace, much of which he had melted down into coin to pay his troops, for Alexander was very generous in sharing the plunder of conquest with his men. By early 330 B.C. the king was on the road again. This time his goal was Persepolis, the religious and ceremonial capital of the Persian Empire and its wealthiest city.

The Destruction of Persepolis

In Persepolis, the very heart of the Achaemenid Empire, Alexander would not be welcomed as a liberator as he had been in Babylon or Egypt. Approaching the city, his troops met with fierce opposition from Persian defenders. The army also had a disturbing encounter with some recently freed Greek and Macedonian prisoners who had been horribly mutilated by their Persian captors, some with their noses and ears cut off, others missing their hands. Alexander immediately proposed to return the men to Europe, but they declined his offer, saying that their grotesque appearance would make them outcasts in their own

"Alexander the cursed"

The ancient Persians' hatred for Alexander in the wake of his savage destruction of their holiest city Persepolis is evident in a Persian text from the era that purports to be a prophecy about a violent conqueror who would arrive in Asia from the west, a conqueror who bears a striking resemblance to the Macedonian king. The alleged oracle is quoted in Michael Wood's In the Footsteps of Alexander the Great:

> One day there shall come into the rich lands of Asia an unbelieving man,
> Wearing on his shoulders a purple cloak,
> Savage, fiery, a stranger to justice. For a thunderbolt raised him up,
> Though he is but a man. All Asia shall suffer a yoke of evil,
> And its soaked earth shall drink much blood.
> But even so Hades shall attend him even though he knows it not:
> And in the end those whom he wished to destroy,
> By them he and his race be destroyed.

"This tradition of Alexander," writes Wood, "has never died out in Persia, and it is still maintained by the keepers of the old religion in Persia—the Zoroastrians." Even today, these descendants of the worshippers of the ancient Persian god Ahura Mazda have not forgiven Alexander, as one member of a Zoroastrian congregation revealed to Wood when the British author visited Iran in the 1990s:

> He may be the Great to the Greeks, and to you Europeans, but we call him a devil. This is because he burned down our temples, killed our priests; . . . he destroyed our most precious holy book . . . the Avesta, which was written on 12,000 calf skins in letters of gold. So, why should we call him Great? To us he is a devil. For this reason we call him Iskander Gujaste. Alexander the Accursed.

homeland. Moved to tears by their plight, Alexander showered the former captives with money and provisions and promised them farming and grazing land of their own in Persia.

When Alexander and his forces at last reached the Persian capital, for the first time since the fall of Gaza Alexander gave his soldiers free rein to sack the city. According to Diodorus, the vengeance wrought by Alexander's men on the people of Persepolis was horrific: "The Macedonians raced into it killing all the men and looting the residences. . . . And the women they dragged off, clothes and all, turning captives into slaves. And so, as Persepolis had exceeded all other cities in prosperity, so in the same measure it now exceeded all in misery."[72] While his soldiers were killing, raping, and looting, Alexander ransacked the opulent royal palace. In its enormous strong rooms, he discovered 120,000 gold talents—the equivalent of billions of U.S. dollars today. "Into Alexander's hands," writes Michael Wood, "had fallen the greatest treasure in history."[73] Weighing in at more than seven thousand tons, Alexander's booty from Persepolis, along with the gold and silver he had taken from Susa and Babylon, required no fewer than ten thousand pairs of mules and five thousand camels to carry it off, reports Plutarch. Alexander had inherited substantial debts from his father when he first ascended the Macedonian throne; now, just five years later, he had become the richest man on earth.

One of the most controversial events of Alexander's career occurred in Persepolis toward the end of his stay there in the spring of 330 B.C.: the torching of the vast palace complex, which as the chief residence of the Great King—the "Chosen One" of the supreme Persian god, Ahura Mazda—was also the empire's spiritual center. Some of Alexander's early biographers claim that the fire was an accident, the result of a wild, drunken party. But recent archaeo-logical findings indicate that the inferno that razed the magnificent complex of palaces and audience halls in Persepolis was deliberately set. Alexander's motive for this colossal act of vandalism remains a mystery. Some scholars speculate that he wanted to punish and intimidate the city's Persian aristocracy for failing to acknowledge him as Darius's rightful successor; others believe that he was avenging the Persians' long-ago burning of Athens's holy places.

Whatever Alexander's reasons for destroying the royal complex at Persepolis may have actually been, his Macedonian troops likely viewed the spectacular fire as a "fitting climax to one victorious expedition,"[74] writes a historian. With the entire Persian heartland under Alexander's control, add Fildes and Fletcher, "they must have expected that soon they would be returning home in triumph."[75] In fact, though Alexander would soon demobilize his troops from the Greek states of the League of Corinth, he had no intention whatsoever of releasing the Macedonians who made up the bulk of his army. With the enormous wealth of Persia now his, Alexander could finance any campaign of conquest he wanted—even to the farthest reaches of the known world. At Gordium the gods had decreed that he would rule over all of Asia, and Alexander was determined to fulfill his destiny. Alexander's—and his unsuspecting army's—epic trek eastward was just beginning.

Chapter Five

DESPOT

During the four years following the burning of the royal palace at Persepolis in 330 B.C., Alexander led his army eastward to the remotest reaches of the former Persian Empire. Pressing on across snow-capped peaks and scorching deserts, Alexander and his men would traverse thousands of miles of uncharted and treacherous terrain. Along the way, Alexander and his long-suffering Macedonian troops would find themselves increasingly at odds over the king's apparently insatiable appetite for conquest and his growing tendency toward Persian-style autocracy.

Hunting Down Darius and Bessus

Soon after razing Persepolis, Alexander was informed that Darius was hiding out in his palace at Ecbatana (modern Hamadan, Iran). Grimly determined to dispose of his competitor for the Persian throne once and for all, Alexander raced northward toward Ecbatana, pushing his soldiers so hard through the blazing summer heat "that many of the men, unable to stand the pace, dropped out, and a number of horses were worked to death,"[76] reports Arrian. A few days' march from his destination, Alexander learned that Darius, along with a small entourage including his cousin Bessus, had already fled the city. Intelligence reports indicated that they were headed for the empire's remote northeastern province of Bactria (modern-day northern Afghanistan). Continuing on, Alexander and his weary troops finally came upon what appeared to be

Darius's abandoned baggage train near Hecatompylos, just north of present-day Tehran, Iran.

Inside one of the wagons, the Macedonians made a grisly discovery: the bloody corpse of the Great King himself. With Alexander and his troops closing in on them, Darius's entourage had renounced the king in favor of his kinsman Bessus, a veteran cavalry commander and the satrap of Bactria. When Darius insisted that he would rather face Alexander than continue on to Bactria in the company of traitors, Bessus and his followers ran

the king through with their spears before escaping into the desert.

For Alexander, notes Pierre Briant, "Darius' murder was a great political windfall. After Darius' death Alexander portrayed himself as the Great King's avenger—rather than usurper [someone who seizes power without legal right]."[77] Alexander made a point of treating Darius's body with the utmost respect, ordering that it be sent to Persepolis for a magnificent royal burial in traditional Achaemenid style. Then he set off at top speed for the rugged hills of Bactria to hunt down Darius's

Alexander kneels over the body of Darius after the Persian king's own men murdered him. Alexander treated the king's corpse with utmost respect.

Alexander's army discovers Bessus bound to a yoke, betrayed by one of his own allies. Alexander had Bessus tried on charges of regicide and publicly executed.

killer and his newest rival for the Persian throne, Bessus, or King Artaxerxes IV, as the late monarch's cousin was now calling himself.

Alexander and his army pursued Bessus through the desolate northern frontiers of the old Persian Empire for more than a year. They traveled from the snowy mountains of the Hindu Kush to the scorching plains of Sogdiana (modern Uzbekistan and Tajikistan); along the way, many of Alexander's men succumbed to frostbite and heatstroke. When the hard-pressed Macedonian army's food supplies ran out,

they even had to slaughter their work animals. Finally, in the summer of 329 B.C., Bessus was betrayed by one of his own allies, the Sogdian baron Spitamenes, who tied up the would-be monarch and left him for Alexander's army to find. As determined as ever to present himself as Darius's avenger and rightful successor, after ordering that Bessus be tortured in the customary Achaemenid manner by having his ears and nose cut off, Alexander had his rival sent off to Ecbatana for trial before an assembly of Persian nobles on charges of regicide (the killing of a king) and treason. A few months later Bessus was publicly executed, either by crucifixion or dismemberment—the ancient histories differ as to the exact method of death.

A Revolt and a Royal Marriage

Although Bessus was no longer a threat, the Macedonians' grueling military campaign in central Asia was not yet over. After handing over Bessus to Alexander, Spitamenes suddenly decided to recruit his own army in Sogdiana with the intention of freeing the northeastern provinces of the former Achaemenid Empire from Macedonian rule. It would take Alexander nearly two years to crush Spitamenes, one of

Alexander and His Image

From the beginning of his career, Alexander was preoccupied with how other people viewed him. "Alexander the Great was a skilled propagandist and was fully aware of the power of the image in a world in which few were literate," write Alan Fildes and Joann Fletcher in their book *Alexander the Great: Son of the Gods*. "Throughout his reign," the authors contend, "he maintained close control over his own official portraiture, be it sculpted, painted, or carved."

The sculptor Lysippus created this and other flattering busts of Alexander the Great.

According to Plutarch, the only sculptor Alexander believed was good enough to portray him was the celebrated Greek artist Lysippus. One reason why Alexander, who was reputed to be stocky and short in stature, may have preferred Lysippus above all other sculptors is that Lysippus typically made his subjects look taller and more slender than they were in real life. Alexander's favorite painter, Apelles, also tended to portray his subjects in a highly flattering light. In one of his better-known works, Apelles even painted Alexander wielding a thunderbolt in the style of Zeus, the most powerful of the Greek gods.

In 327 B.C. Alexander married Roxane, the daughter of the Sogdian chief Oxyartes. Alexander's decision to take a foreign bride dismayed many of his followers.

the most cunning and determined adversaries he would encounter in his Asian campaign. Alexander's response to Spitamenes' treachery and the rebellion in Sogdiana "was at once desperate and ruthless," write Alan Fildes and Joann Fletcher; "his soldiers massacred the adult male inhabitants of each defeated stronghold and enslaved the women and children."[78]

In early 327 B.C., with the Macedonians finally closing in on Spitamenes, one of his panic-stricken allies turned on the rebel leader and brought his severed head to Alexander as a token of good faith. Shortly after, Alexander captured the mountain stronghold of another of Spitamenes' former allies, the Sogdian chieftain Oxyartes. Among the captives was Oxyartes' daughter Roxane, whose exceptional beauty reportedly made a deep impression on the twenty-eight-year-old king. "Alexander fell in love with her at first sight; but, captive though she was, he refused, for all his passion, to force her to his will, and condescended to marry her,"[79] asserts Arrian. Whatever Alexander's actual feelings for Roxane may have been, his marriage to the young noblewoman in a traditional Sogdian ceremony was an astute political move, a means of forging an invaluable alliance with the powerful and defiant aristocracy of the northeastern provinces.

Yet, while Alexander's marriage to Roxane helped reconcile his onetime enemies in Sogdiana and Bactria to his rule, it did not sit well with his Macedonian followers. Already disgruntled by the long and arduous central Asian campaign, many of Alexander's veteran troops were dismayed by their king's decision to wed an outsider. They viewed Alexander's decision to marry an Asian as just another step in their leader's "orientalization," his abandonment of traditional Macedonian and Greek ways in favor of Eastern dress, manners, and political practices.

Alexander's Growing Rift with the Macedonians

Alexander had begun to show what many of his Macedonian followers considered an undue partiality toward Asians—and particularly the former Persian ruling class—as early as 332–331 B.C. during his peaceful takeovers of Egypt and Babylon. Eager to preserve Egypt's and Babylon's efficiently run bureaucracies, Alexander had awarded Egypt's Persian satrap an important post in the kingdom's new government and even allowed Babylon's longtime Persian governor, Mazaeus, to stay on as satrap. As he moved eastward through the Persian heartland and into central Asia, Alexander relied more and more on experienced Persian officials to help him rule his ever-expanding empire. The king's trust in the old Persian ruling class had its limits, however: Alexander invariably kept local military garrisons and treasuries firmly in Macedonian hands.

The Cities of Alexander the Great

During the course of his conquest of the old Achaemenid Empire, Alexander founded as many as seventy new cities on the Asian continent, naming the majority of them after himself. Most of the remaining cities he named after fallen companions, including his beloved warhorse Bucephalas. Bucephalas died shortly after Alexander's fierce battle with the forces of the Indian raja Porus near the Hydaspes (modern Jhelum) River. In honor of the stallion he had first tamed as a boy some two decades earlier, Alexander created Bucephala on the banks of the Jhelum.

Most of the cities that Alexander founded—with a few notable exceptions such as Alexandria-in-Egypt and Alexandretta (now Iskenderun, Turkey)—were in the central and eastern portions of the old Persian Empire. Some, including Alexandria-in-Egypt and Alexandria-Charax between the Tigris and Eulaeus rivers, were clearly meant to become major trading centers. The majority of the settlements, however, were intended primarily to serve as defensive sites and were heavily garrisoned. For example, Alexander stationed nearly five thousand infantry and cavalry in Alexandria-in-Arachosia (now Kandahar, Afghanistan), one of the first cities that he founded in the rebellious northeastern fringes of his new domain.

As he fought his way through central Asia, Alexander's decision to supplement his forces with Sogdian and Bactrian conscripts also angered many of his Macedonian veterans. The Macedonians were particularly incensed when Alexander established an ambitious program to prepare Asian boys for service in his army, for which he drafted thirty thousand Persian and other native youths in the conquered lands. As part of the new program, the young recruits were to be taught Greek and coached in Macedonian military techniques. Although Alexander had very practical reasons for instituting the training program, including his expectation that the boys would serve "as hostages for the good behavior of their compatriots at home,"[80] note scholars A.B. Bosworth and E.J. Baynham, much of the Macedonian rank-and-file saw the scheme as another example of their king's inexplicable fondness for a people whom they disdained as their enemies and inferiors.

In addition to his willingness to integrate Asians into his administration and army, many Macedonians decried what they considered their king's growing attachment to Eastern customs during the central Asian campaign. By the time of his marriage to Roxane, Alexander had already adopted many of the traditional articles of dress of the Persian royalty. According to Plutarch, donning the long robes and *kyrbasia* (pointed caps) of the Achaemenid monarchs was for Alexander a matter of policy, a pragmatic means of associating "himself with local customs, on the grounds that the sight of what is familiar and congenial goes a long way towards winning people over."[81] For many of his men,

however, Alexander's adoption of Persian royal garb was just one more sign of his drift away from his Macedonian roots.

Murder and Conspiracy

During the course of his long campaign in the northeastern fringes of the old Achaemenid Empire, Alexander's personality as well as his appearance underwent drastic changes. The conqueror became increasingly short-tempered and suspicious of those around him,

Alexander grieves the death of his longtime friend Cleitus. The conqueror himself murdered his dear friend in a drunken rage.

interpreting any criticism of his behavior as evidence of disloyalty. He also began drinking more heavily, a weakness that would lead to one of the most notorious episodes of his entire career: the murder of his cavalry commander and longtime friend, Cleitus.

Cleitus's death occurred in 328 B.C. at a huge drinking banquet hosted by Alexander for his Macedonian officers and associates at Maracanda (modern-day Samarkand). During the festivities, some of the most extravagant flatterers in the king's entourage declared that Alexander's achievements far outstripped anything his father, King Philip, had done, even claiming that his triumphs matched those of the Greek hero turned god Heracles. According to Arrian, this was too much for Cleitus, who "for some time past had quite obviously deprecated [condemned] the change in Alexander: he liked neither his move towards the manners of the East, nor the sycophantic [flattering] expressions of his courtiers."[82] Cleitus argued that Alexander's victories were not personal triumphs but, rather, the achievement of the Macedonians as a whole. Adding insult to injury, Cleitus then began to glorify Philip's achievements and put down Alexander's. In a fit of drunken rage, Alexander seized a spear from one of his attendants and struck his friend dead. Immediately, the king was filled with remorse. For three days he grieved, spurning all food and wine.

Alexander was finally brought out of his depression by a court philosopher who assured his master that since every action performed by a king is just, Alexander should not reproach himself for Cleitus's death. The philosopher "may have alleviated the king's pain with this kind of argument," contends Plutarch, "but he also considerably increased his conceit and his inclination to disregard rules."[82]

Soon after Cleitus's murder, Alexander found himself embroiled in a new dispute with his Macedonian followers, this one centering on a traditional Persian practice called *proskynesis* (prostration). According to Persian custom, anyone entering the presence of the Great King was supposed to cast himself face down on the ground as a show of subservience. Alexander's Persian courtiers had adopted this practice with him from the beginning, but in early 327 B.C. Alexander started trying to impose it on his Macedonian associates as well. The king's compatriots detested the new policy; according to Macedonian and Greek tradition, prostration was appropriate only before a statue of a god and never before a human being. Even Callisthenes, Alexander's chief propagandist and one of his most blatant flatterers, loudly criticized the king's new decree. In an impassioned speech before his countrymen, Callisthenes argued that it was "outrageous" for Alexander to expect such subservience from Macedonians and Greeks; prostra-

Alexander and the Naked Philosophers of Taxila

While Alexander was in Taxila in modern-day Pakistan, he was intrigued by reports of a group of native sages whom the Macedonians called "Gymnosophists." Renouncing even the most basic comforts of life, including clothing, they lived in the countryside just outside of the city. According to Arrian, Alexander happened to come upon a group of Gymnosophists one day in an open meadow,

where they used to meet to discuss philosophy. On the appearance of Alexander and his army, these venerable men stamped with their feet and gave no other sign of interest. Alexander asked them through interpreters what they meant by this odd behavior, and they replied: "King Alexander, every man can possess only so much of the earth's surface as this we are standing on. You are but human like the rest of us, save that you are always busy and up to no good, traveling so many miles from your home, a nuisance to yourself and to others. Ah well! You will soon be dead, and then you will own just as much of this earth as will suffice to bury you."

Arrian notes dryly that although Alexander publicly praised the naked philosophers of Taxila for their "sage words," in "point of fact his conduct was always the exact opposite of what he then professed to admire."

tion before a man, he said, was a practice "fit only for barbarians."[84]

Ultimately, Alexander abandoned his unpopular experiment with *proskynesis*, but he never forgave Callisthenes for his role in the scheme's failure. According to Arrian, in the wake of the *proskynesis* controversy, Alexander was constantly on the lookout for any chance to discredit his campaign's official historian. His opportunity was not long in coming. During the winter of 327 B.C., one of the royal pages, an adolescent named Hermolaus, resentful over what he considered an unjust

whipping, masterminded a plot to murder Alexander while he slept. (Royal pages, the sons of Macedonian noblemen, performed a number of services for the king, including guarding his tent at night.) When Alexander got wind of the conspiracy, he had Hermolaus and the other pages who had plotted with him tortured. While they were on the rack, the boys said that Callisthenes, who served as the royal pages' tutor, had asked them to commit the crime. Despite their young age, the pages were punished for their treachery by being stoned to death. The ancient sources disagree as to Callisthenes' fate. Some claim that he was tortured and then hanged; others say that he was dragged around in chains by the army until he died. However Callisthenes met his end, his death, along with the murder of Cleitus, "made it clear that it was perilous for anyone to disagree with the king in public,"[85] notes one scholar. Public criticism of Alexander by his Macedonian inner circle appears to have been rare from this time on.

To India

By 327 B.C. the year of the so-called Pages' Conspiracy, Alexander and his army had trekked thousands of miles. They had marched through virtually every part of the vast Achaemenid Empire with one notable exception: the fabled land of India. Although his Macedonian troops were weary of campaigning and anxious to return to their homes and families, Alexander was determined to push on to that exotic and faraway country. "Alexander's horizon of conquest was continually expanding," writes Green. "Macedon, for him, had begun to seem very small. . . . He would not, could not, abandon the vision of glory and empire that drove him on."[86]

During the late 500s B.C., King Darius I had conquered the territory that Alexander and his fellow Macedonians knew as "India" but which today is almost entirely contained within the republic of Pakistan—the so-called Punjab region

of the Indus River and its tributaries. Over the course of the next two centuries, however, Persian authority steadily dwindled in the distant Punjab. By the time Alexander launched his Indian campaign in mid-327 B.C., several powerful native rajas (kings) dominated the territory of the upper Indus and its branches, the Hydaspes (modern Jhelum), Acesines (modern Chenab), Hydraotes (modern Ravi), and Hyphasis (modern Beas). Alexander, having no concept of the true size of India—or of the very existence of China—believed that by conquering these kingdoms of the Punjab, he would be winning not only India for his empire but all of the Asian continent to the shores of the great "Eastern Ocean" (the Pacific).

In the summer of 327, Alexander set out from Bactria for India with his largest and most diverse army to date: some seventy-five thousand men, including tens of thousands of Bactrians, Sogdians, and other natives of his new Asian empire. Traveling with the soldiers were perhaps another forty thousand noncombatants, including camel drivers, muleteers, peddlers, and the wives, mistresses, and children of the troops. The journey turned out to be an arduous one for Alexander's troops and thousands of camp followers. The mountainous terrain was treacherous, and the peoples of the Afghan-Pakistani borderlands were extraordinarily fierce fighters. Characteristically, Alexander did not hesitate to savagely crush the defiant cities and tribes. At the chief city of the region, Massaga, Alexander ruthlessly ordered the massacre of seven thousand Indian mercenaries whom he had earlier pledged to spare, "an action which Plutarch regarded as one of the greatest stains on his military career,"[87] writes Richard Stoneman.

In the spring of 326 B.C., nearly a year after leaving Bactria, Alexander finally crossed the Indus River and entered Taxila in modern Pakistan. There he was met by the local raja, Ambhi, who promised Alexander five thousand troops in return for his assistance against Ambhi's chief rival, Porus, the ruler of the territory between the Hydaspes and Acesines rivers. Alexander readily accepted Ambhi's offer and was just starting out for Porus's kingdom when he received word that Porus was waiting for him at the Hydaspes with an army of fifty thousand troops, three hundred chariots, and two hundred war elephants. Alexander and his men were about to encounter one of the most awesome enemy forces of the entire Asian campaign.

The Macedonian phalanx advances on Porus's troops near the Hydaspes River in 326 B.C. Alexander's men achieved a decisive victory over the Indian forces.

The Battle of the Hydaspes River

From his defensive position on the left bank of the Hydaspes, Porus, who stood nearly seven feet tall according to some ancient accounts, watched closely as Alexander's army approached the river. According to Caroline Alexander, Alexander was "determined to create as much confusion as possible"; he ordered that campfires be lit erratically and "drilled his men up and down the riverbank as if preparing for action. . . . To the watching Indians, the Macedonians seemed to be perpetually on the brink of decisive action. Eventually tiring of false alarms, Porus pulled many of his night watches, and Alexander saw his opportunity."[88] On a dark and stormy night, the Macedonian commander led his army across the river at a secluded and heavily wooded spot about fifteen miles upstream from where Porus's imposing force was assembled.

In the fierce battle that ensued, Porus counted on his three hundred highly trained charioteers and two-hundred-strong elephant tank corps to carry the day for the Indian army. Although the chariots quickly became mired in the rain-soaked soil of the battlefield, the elephant corps proved considerably more effective against Alexander's terrified troops. Writes one ancient historian, "Seized around the waists by the elephants' trunks and tossed into the air, some soldiers met a horrible death. Many others also met

their deaths, thrust through by the animals' tusks, their bodies pierced by wounds."[89] The tide began to turn, however, after Alexander ordered his troops to aim their arrows at the mahouts (elephant drivers) and strike at the tender parts of the elephants' bodies with their pikes. The wounded and riderless animals started to rush about wildly. In the confusion, the frenzied beasts trampled more Indians than enemy troops, and Porus's army launched a panicked retreat. Porus himself, who had fought bravely alongside his men throughout the long and bloody battle, agreed to surrender only after suffering a debilitating shoulder wound.

When the raja was brought before Alexander, the Macedonian conqueror was deeply impressed by his opponent's courage and regal bearing. According to Arrian, Porus, who had lost two sons in the battle, had only one request of Alexander: that he be treated like a king. Delighted by Porus's dignity and spirit, Alexander restored all of his territory with the stipulation that the raja remain loyal to him. "The ancient authors point again and again to Alexander's generosity in allowing Porus to keep his crown and his kingdom,"[90] observes Pierre Briant. In fact, leaving Porus in charge of his old kingdom made a great deal of political sense, Briant and other modern historians contend, since Alexander lacked the manpower to control this vast, distant region himself.

Porus surrenders to Alexander at the Hydaspes River. After demanding an oath of loyalty from Porus, Alexander restored the raja's territory.

With an army reinforced by five thousand of the raja's best troops and dozens of his war elephants, Alexander departed Porus's kingdom and continued his march eastward into "India" (modern northeastern Pakistan) during the spring and summer of 326 B.C. Crossing the Acesines and Hydraotes rivers, he subdued numerous cities and towns along the way. "Only when he reached the banks of the Hyphasis," writes Briant, "did he learn the unpleasant truth about the region he planned to conquer."[91] According to a local ruler, beyond the Hyphasis lay the scorching Thar Desert and then another river, the wide and perilous Ganges. On the other side of the Ganges, the ruler reported, Alexander and his men would encounter the army of the raja of Magadha, a huge force that supposedly included four thousand war elephants and two thousand chariots. Despite these dire warnings, Alexander remained grimly resolved to cross the Hyphasis and continue his drive eastward. He was not about to give up on his glorious dream of conquering all of Asia, right to the edge of the legendary Eastern Ocean, which he was sure lay just a short march beyond the Ganges. But Alexander was in for a bitter surprise. On the muddy banks of the rain-swollen Hyphasis, for the first time ever, his troops challenged their commander's orders.

Chapter Six

An Untimely Death and an Enduring Fame

The last two years of Alexander's life were in many ways a low point for the king: He was forced to abandon his campaign to conquer all of Asia after his weary soldiers finally rebelled, and his health was irreparably damaged by a serious wound and his increasingly heavy drinking. Yet long after his untimely death at the age of thirty-two, the Macedonian conqueror's influence and fame would live on.

Mutiny at the Hyphasis River

By the time they reached the banks of the Hyphasis River in the summer of 326 B.C., Alexander and his troops had endured more than two months of torrential rain and oppressive heat. It was the height of the monsoon season, and the nearly incessant downpours took a heavy toll on the army. Serious illness-es, particularly malaria and dysentery, spread through the camp; food and clothing became moldy; and weapons and armor rusted. Worst of all were the hordes of poisonous snakes that invaded the soldiers' tents in search of dry ground; many men suffered excruciating deaths after being bitten. When rumors began to circulate that a huge Indian army, including thousands of war elephants, awaited them on the other side of the Ganges, Alexander's men decided that they had had enough: they would not march another mile eastward.

Alexander, convinced that the shores of the legendary Eastern Ocean—and the edge of the Asian continent—were just a short march away, was enraged. For three days he shut himself away in his tent, sulking.

Nonetheless, the army refused to budge. The stalemate finally ended after Alexander commanded his official soothsayer to determine what the gods wanted him to do by consulting the omens. Conveniently, the omens indicated that Alexander should abandon his advance eastward and return to Susa and Babylon. Still furious but with his pride intact, the king announced that he would abide by the gods' wishes. After constructing twelve gigantic stone altars at the edge of the Hyphasis to mark the eastern limit of his Asian conquests, the army was to begin the long journey back.

Although Alexander's troops were overjoyed by his proclamation, their ordeal was far from over. Determined to explore and conquer southern "India" (modern southeastern Pakistan), Alexander planned to take a new—and roundabout—route back to Persia proper. First, the army would follow the Indus River all the way south to the Indian Ocean. Only after reaching the coast of the Arabian Sea would they veer westward toward the Persian heartland, a route that would take them straight through the Gedrosian desert, one of the most desolate regions in the world.

Crossing the Gedrosia

By November 326 B.C. Alexander's troops had constructed a fleet of ships and begun their journey down the Indus. For nine months, they fought their way toward the Indian coast, conquering dozens of towns and slaughtering thousands of natives along the way. The fiercest resistance came from the warlike Malli people. During the ferocious battle to take the chief Mallian city—present-day Multan, Pakistan—Alexander was gravely wounded when his lung was pierced by an arrow. Alexander survived, but the unfortunate inhabitants of Multan did not. In revenge for their commander's injury, Alexander's troops massacred every man, woman, and child in the city.

During the summer of 325 B.C., Alexander's army finally reached the head of the Indus delta. Near present-day Karachi, the king divided his forces, ordering a fleet under his friend Nearchus to return westward by sea along the coast of the Indian Ocean. Meanwhile, he would lead the bulk of the army back toward Susa and Babylon by way of the vast Gedrosian desert, which straddles modern Pakistan and Iran. According to Nearchus, Alexander's primary reason for taking this notoriously hazardous route was a desire to match the exploits of the one ruler reputed to have successfully brought an army through the barren Gedrosia: Semiramis, the legendary warrior-queen of Babylon.

Alexander's determination not to be outdone by his famous predecessor resulted in massive hardship and suffering for his followers. Although the Gedrosian campaign started out well, drinkable water soon became scarce, provisions ran dangerously low, and the summer sun beat down mercilessly on the weary troops and camp followers as they trudged through the desert's rugged terrain. "Sometimes they met with lofty hills of sand—loose, deep sand, into which they sank as if it were mud or untrodden snow; sometimes, climbing or descending, the mules and horses suffered even greater distress from the uneven and treacherous sur-face of the track,"[92] Arrian reports. Tens of thousands of marchers succumbed to exhaustion, heatstroke, dehydration, or starvation; those who fell ill were simply left to die. No one "could give them a helping hand," writes Arrian, "no one could stay behind to ease their sufferings, for the essential thing was to get on with all possible speed, and the effort to save the army as a whole inevitably took precedence over the suffering of

Alexander's "Riotous" Journey Through Carmania

After Alexander and his army finally emerged from the Gedrosian desert, they celebrated their safe return in time-honored Macedonian fashion by setting out on what Plutarch describes in his Greek Lives *as a "riotous seven-day journey through Carmania" (the region between Gedrosia and the Persian heartland). According to Plutarch, Alexander, who drank continuously on the journey, was*

> pulled along at an easy pace by eight horses, on a dais [throne] fixed on a tall, conspicuous, oblong scaffold. . . . He was followed by an enormous train of wagons. . . . These carts carried the rest of his friends and officers of his army, all of whom . . . were drinking. There was not a shield or helmet or pike to be seen, but all the way along the road there were soldiers ladling wine out of huge jars and . . . drinking to one another's health, some doing so even when they marched along, others lying by the side of the road.

One ancient historian who was thoroughly disgusted by Alexander's wine-sodden trek through Carmania was Quintus Curtius Rufus. Fewer than a thousand sober men, he speculated, could have overcome the Macedonian revelers, but as usual, fortune was on Alexander's side and none of his Persian subjects tried to ambush the inebriated conqueror and his army as they wended their way westward. Fortune, the Roman historian noted dryly, "allots fame and a price to things, and she turned even this piece of disgraceful soldiering into a glorious achievement!"

individual men."[93] Although the exact death toll is unknown, according to some accounts, more of Alexander's troops perished in the Gedrosian desert than died in all the battles the Macedonians had fought since arriving in Asia eight years earlier. Some eighty thousand soldiers and camp followers are believed to have accompanied Alexander into the desert; as few as twenty thousand may have survived the two-month-long crossing.

If Nearchus is to be believed, it was Alexander's overweening pride that spurred him to jeopardize his own life and those of his troops by choosing the desert route in the first place. Nevertheless, many of the ancient historians asserted that one of the king's most heroic deeds occurred during the deadly Gedrosian campaign. According to Arrian's version of the episode, one day as the parched forces trudged on, a soldier came upon a trickle of water that had collected in a shallow gully. Scooping up the water in his helmet, he offered it to his commander. Determined to share in all his men's hardships, rather than ride his horse the king had been "marching on foot at the head of his men," and "like everyone else, was tormented by thirst," reports Arrian. Even so, "Alexander, with a word of thanks for the gift, took the helmet and, in full view of his troops, poured the water on the ground." The king's message was clear: If his men could not drink, then neither would he.

"So extraordinary was the effect of this action that the water wasted by Alexander was as good as a drink for every man in the army," writes Arrian. "I cannot praise this act too highly; it was proof, if anything was, not only of his power of endurance, but also of his genius for leadership."[94]

A Mass Marriage

Sixty days after entering the Gedrosian desert, Alexander's greatly depleted force limped into Pura, the capital of the province of Gedrosia. Traveling on to the neighboring region of Carmania, they met up with Nearchus's fleet in December 325 B.C. near the Persian Gulf. A few months later, the reunited army arrived in Susa. There, in the magnificent winter capital of the old Achaemenid Empire, Alexander presided over an extraordinary and controversial ceremony.

In March 324 B.C. Alexander held a huge feast at Susa's royal palace to celebrate his conquest of the Persian Empire. The highlight of the festivities was a lavish wedding ceremony at which Alexander and ninety-two of his Macedonian officers wed Persian noblewomen. The king's bride was none other than Barsine (also known as Stateira), the eldest daughter of Darius III. Alexander ordered his closest friend, Hephaestion, to wed Darius's younger daughter so that the children of his lifelong comrade would be his own nieces and nephews. Two of

Alexander and his Macedonian officers celebrate during the marriage feast at Susa's royal palace. The conqueror had ninety-two of his men married to Persian noblewomen.

the king's other close friends and leading generals, Ptolemy and Seleucus, also married women from the Persian royal family at his behest.

In the past, some scholars viewed Alexander's determination to unite his Macedonian officers with Persian wives as evidence of a broad-minded commitment to the "brotherhood of man." Today, however, most historians assume that Alexander's matchmaking scheme had far more to do with pragmatic political goals than with an idealistic belief in the unity of humankind. In

truth, Alexander did not promote marriages between his court and just any Asian women: Every one of his officers' brides at Susa belonged to the Persian aristocracy. Alexander seems to have believed that a close alliance between his Macedonian inner circle and the traditional Persian ruling class was the best way to retain power in the immense and diverse empire he had conquered. J.R. Hamilton agrees that Alexander's chief motive for the Susa weddings—and for using high-born Persians in his administration and

The Death of Hephaestion

In the summer of 324 B.C. Alexander and his court, including his closest companion since childhood, Hephaestion, journeyed to Ecbatana, where the climate was cooler than in Susa. Every evening, in accordance with Macedonian custom, the king hosted lavish banquets at which everyone consumed copious amounts of undiluted wine. During one of these drinking parties, Hephaestion fell ill with a fever. According to Plutarch, the ailing Hephaestion ignored his doctor's instructions and continued to drink heavily. One day, after consuming "a large cooler of wine" with his "morning meal," Plutarch writes, Hephaestion took a turn for the worse and "died a short while later."

Alexander was devastated by the death of his best friend. Imitating his hero Achilles at the death of his comrade Patroclus, Alexander cut off his hair over the corpse and even decreed that the tails and manes of his horses be shorn as a symbol of mourning. Accusing the hapless doctor of providing his friend with inadequate medical care, Alexander then commanded that Hephaestion's physician be "impaled on a stake," according to Plutarch.

The king also sent messengers to the oracle of the god Amun at Siwa to ask whether his dead comrade could be worshipped as a deity. The priests of Siwa, to whom Alexander had contributed a great deal of money since his visit to Amun's temple seven years earlier, declined to bestow the rank of a god on Hephaestion. But they tactfully declared that Alexander's friend could be worshipped as a hero and that regular sacrificial rituals could be held in his honor.

Alexander staged an elaborate funeral for Hephaestion, his closest companion.

army—may have been "his perception that the empire was best governed with the cooperation of the ruled and that the Persian nobles were best able to secure this."[95]

A Misunderstanding and a Controversial Decree

Most Macedonians deeply resented the forced marriages at Susa. They were even more disgruntled when the thirty thousand young Asians selected by Alexander several years earlier to receive Macedonian military training and a Greek education arrived in Susa. Now in their late teens and early twenties, the native youths' enthusiasm and abilities earned warm praise from Alexander, who referred to them in public as his "Successors," a title that shocked and angered the king's compatriots. Things came to a head in the summer of 324 B.C. when Alexander announced that he was dismissing ten thousand Macedonian troops, men who either had been disabled in battle or had served their time. Although most of them probably would have welcomed the king's proclamation under other circumstances, in the wake of the mass marriages and the Successors controversy, the jealous and resentful Macedonian veterans grumbled that Alexander "had first worn them down with every kind of active service, and now was turning them away in disgrace."[96] They "asked him why he did not send them all away

and regard all Macedonians as useless" now that he had his young Asian soldiers to "help him sweep across the world and bring it all under his control,"[97] reports Plutarch.

Alexander was incensed by what he regarded as the Macedonians' ingratitude. They had all gained substantial treasure from the Asian campaign, he pointed out, and furthermore, Macedonians still held most of the high offices in his administration and all of the top posts in his army. Maybe he should send the lot of them home to Macedon, he threatened, and fill his army's ranks with Persians. Thoroughly humbled, the Macedonians pled for forgiveness. The king graciously relented, and he and his men celebrated the end of their quarrel with a huge feast at Opis (near modern Baghdad, Iraq) at which Asians and Europeans were seated together as a symbol of the partnership between the old Persian ruling class and the Macedonian conquerors. The troops abandoned their earlier objections to demobilization, and ten thousand long-standing Macedonian veterans were duly awarded with generous severance allowances and shipped back home.

A few months after the reconciliation banquet at Opis, Alexander issued a startling decree, an edict that some modern scholars have interpreted as a sign of the king's increasing emotional instability. Alexander demanded that the Greek city-states honor him as a

In 331 B.C. priests of the oracle at Siwa hail Alexander as the son of god, encouraging his belief that he was the son of Zeus-Amun.

god. It was not unusual for the Greeks to worship dead heroes like Achilles, but with the possible exception of the great Spartan general Lysander, no living person had ever before been revered as a god in the ancient Greek world. Although appalled by the conqueror's unprecedented demand, most of the city-states diplomatically complied with his new decree. As one Spartan statesman remarked dryly regarding the edict, "Well, let him be a god if he wants to."[98]

As to when Alexander first began believing that he was something more than a mere mortal, historians are divided. Some contend that as far back as his visit to the oracle at Siwa in 331 B.C., Alexander had become convinced that he was the son of the god Zeus-Amun. According to one ancient source, when Alexander entered the temple at Siwa, the Egyptian high priest "greeted him with the words, 'O, paidion' ('Oh, my son'), but mispronounced the Greek as 'O, pai dios,' meaning 'Oh, son of god,' much to Alexander's delight."[99] On several occasions after his pilgrimage to Siwa, Alexander encouraged his flatterers to equate his own exploits with those of the Greek deities, particularly Dionysus and the hero-god Heracles. No one can ever know for certain when Alexander first started to think of himself as a god, but by 324 B.C. when he issued his controversial edict to the city-states of Greece, it is evident that not only did he believe in his own divinity, but he was determined that the rest of the Greek world should recognize his superhuman status as well.

The Death of a Conqueror

Alexander's belief in his divinity and his remarkable military successes seem to have left the conqueror with a conviction that he was invincible, as the priestess at Delphi had called him more than a decade earlier. Although he had never fully recovered from the brutal chest wound he suffered in Multan, by early 323 B.C. Alexander was eager to embark on a glorious and daring new expedition. As Arrian once wrote of the Macedonian king, Alexander the Great had "an insatiable thirst for extending his possessions."[100] His next undertaking, Alexander decided, would be the conquest of Arabia. Alexander's resolve to vanquish Arabia may have been spurred not only by a desire to obtain control of the lucrative Arabian spice trade but by personal motives. According to one of the king's contemporaries, the Arabs "were the only barbarians of this region that had not sent an embassy to [Alexander] or done anything as befits their position and showed respect to him."[101] Never one to take a perceived slight lightly, Alexander decided that the Arabs needed to be punished.

In the spring of 323 B.C., Alexander and his court arrived in Babylon, from which he planned to launch his ambitious new military campaign. At Babylon, Alexander began drinking more heavily than ever. On May 29, following a marathon drinking binge with his Macedonian officers and friends, Alexander developed a high fever. As the days went by, his condition worsened. Finally, Arrian reports, his alarmed soldiers insisted on seeing their leader one last time to say their farewells: "Nothing could keep them from a sight of him, and the motive in almost every heart was grief and a sort of helpless bewilderment at the thought of losing their king. Lying speechless as the men filed by, he yet struggled to raise his head, and in his eyes there was a look of recognition for each individual as he passed."[102] Soon after, on June 10, 323 B.C., Alexander the Great died. He was not quite thirty-three years old.

The precise cause of Alexander's death remains shrouded in mystery. Without question, his health had been gravely weakened by years of strenuous campaigning and excessive alcohol consumption, not to mention the severe wound he received at Multan.

Modern scholars speculate that the king may have succumbed to an infection such as malaria or typhus, both of which cause high fevers and were common in the Middle East at the time, or to liver failure brought on by habitual binge drinking. Immediately after Alexander's death, the rumor spread that the king had been poisoned, possibly by a supporter of the veteran general Antipater, whom Alexander was planning to replace as his deputy in Macedon. There is no firm evidence for this assertion, however, and most historians agree that Alexander likely died from natural causes.

After Alexander

Alexander's sudden death caused enormous uncertainty back in Macedon and throughout his empire. The question was who would succeed him. Alexander had died during the thirteenth year of his reign without ever having designated an heir. Legend says that when his top generals asked him to name his successor, the dying Alexander merely whispered, "the best man."[103]

Two months after Alexander's death, his first wife, Roxane, gave birth to a baby boy, whom she named after his father. Alexander's former generals dutifully appointed the child as co-

Alexander's men crowd around the conqueror's deathbed. The cause of Alexander's untimely death remains a mystery to this day.

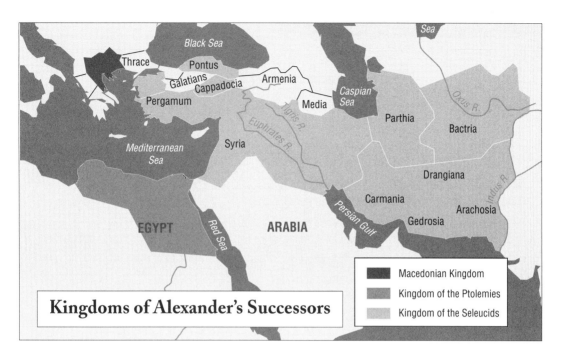

Kingdoms of Alexander's Successors

- Macedonian Kingdom
- Kingdom of the Ptolemies
- Kingdom of the Seleucids

regent of the Macedonian kingdom along with Alexander's mentally disabled half-brother, Philip Arrihidaeus, the illegitimate son of King Philip and one of his numerous mistresses. There was no genuine loyalty to either of the kings among Alexander's old associates, however, and by 310 B.C., both regents had been murdered. Soon after their deaths, Alexander's top commanders, who had divvied up the various regions of their fallen leader's empire among themselves, proclaimed their provinces to be independent realms. Within two decades of Alexander's death, the remarkable empire he had devoted virtually his entire adult life to conquering had fragmented into a host of feuding successor kingdoms.

Yet the disintegration of Alexander's vast empire did not sound the death knell of Macedonian rule in North Africa and western and central Asia. From Egypt and Asia Minor in the west to modern-day Afghanistan and Pakistan in the east, monarchs of Macedonian descent continued to reign for centuries after the conqueror's death. The most illustrious of these dynasties, the ruling house founded in Egypt by Alexander's general Ptolemy, would survive for nearly three hundred years, until the suicide of the famed Cleopatra, the last Greek-speaking ruler in Egypt. Not until 30 B.C. would Ptolemaic Egypt, the longest-lived of the kingdoms created by Alexander's Macedonian successors, succumb to the new superpower of the ancient world: Rome.

Alexander's Missing Mausoleum

Immediately after his death, Alexander's body became an "object of rivalry and symbol of power," writes Richard Stoneman in *Alexander the Great*. Perdiccas, one of Alexander's top generals, took charge of the funeral arrangements, ordering that the king be embalmed and placed in a gold coffin and that a magnificent, bejeweled funeral wagon be constructed. Sixty-four mules were to pull the huge vehicle across Asia toward the Hellespont. Alexander's final resting place, Perdiccas decreed, was to be in Aegae, Macedon, the traditional burial place of the Macedonian royal family.

Alexander's mummified corpse, however, never reached Aegae. Instead, it was kidnapped and diverted to Egypt by Alexander's ambitious general and longtime friend Ptolemy, who had been steadily building his influence in that wealthy kingdom ever since Alexander's death. By laying claim to Alexander's body, Ptolemy sought to present himself as Alexander's legitimate successor in Egypt. Eventually, the king's body ended up in Alexandria, Egypt, where it was placed in an elaborate marble mausoleum.

Over the centuries, several Roman emperors reportedly visited the famed conqueror's tomb in Alexandria. By A.D. 300, however, the mausoleum was gone. Some historians believe that the tomb was razed during the fierce rioting in Alexandria during the late A.D. 200s. For many years, it was widely believed that the mosque of Nabi Daniel was constructed on the site of the demolished mausoleum. Recent archaeological excavations, however, suggest that the royal tombs and palaces of ancient Alexandria lay much farther east than the vicinity of Nabi Daniel. If this proves to be the case, then the fragments of a stately alabaster tomb recently unearthed near an old Greek cemetery in Alexandria's eastern quarter may prove to be part of the great conqueror's final resting place. But for now at least, the mystery of Alexander's lost mausoleum remains unsolved.

Alexander the Great's Legacy

Although the political empire that he created proved fragile, from Egypt in the west to India in the east, Alexander the Great's conquests had an enduring impact on the cultural landscape of the ancient world. The Macedonian successor kingdoms that arose following the king's death provided the framework for a brilliant new epoch: the Hellenistic Age (323–30 B.C.), in which Greek culture spread throughout much of North Africa and Asia. Science, literature, art, and trade flourished as the learning and cultures of East and West mingled. From the shores of the Mediterranean to the banks of the Hyphasis River, Greek emerged as the universal language used by merchants, educators, and government officials. For hundreds of years after Alexander's death, the dominance of the Greek language in the lands he had conquered eased the spread of new ideas. Richard Stoneman writes, for example, that the spread of Christianity during the early first millennium A.D. "could hardly be imagined without the conquests of Alexander the Great."[104]

In the past, many historians believed that, inspired by his tutor Aristotle, Alexander embarked on his Asian expedition with the express intention of spreading Greek learning and culture throughout the East. Today, however, most scholars would agree with J.R. Hamilton that,

> While Greek culture followed in the wake of Alexander's conquest, Alexander himself had no such mission. . . . No one will dispute

Alexander's funeral procession as shown in a nineteenth-century engraving.

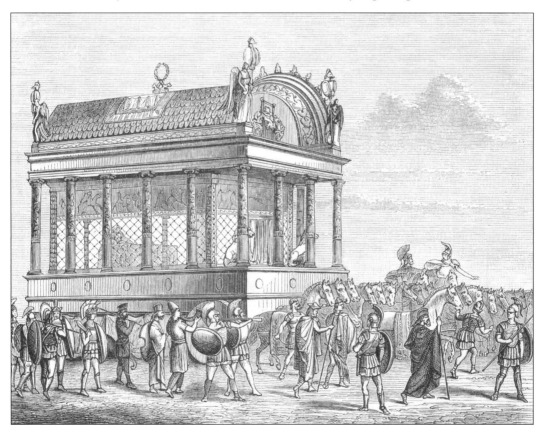

that the inhabitants of Asia (or at least the upper strata among them) were to some extent Hellenized as a result of Alexander's conquests, but that is a very different matter from saying that Alexander consciously aimed at promoting this.[105]

Above all else, Alexander the Great seems to have been motivated in his remarkable career of conquest by an overwhelming desire for personal glory and eternal fame of the sort that his hero Achilles enjoyed. While opinion regarding the fundamental nobility or villainy of Alexander the Great has remained divided over the years, few would dispute the king's success in achieving lasting fame. Although the fame Alexander the Great sought so determinedly throughout his life, unlike that of the legendary Achilles, may not yet prove "eternal," as the nearly fifteen hundred books and articles that have been published on the Macedonian conqueror in the past century and a half alone attest, it has managed to endure—and even to grow—over the more than two millennia since his death.

NOTES

Chapter 1: A Warrior-King in Training

1. Richard Stoneman, *Alexander the Great.* New York: Routledge, 1997, p. 10.
2. Quoted in Caroline Alexander, "Alexander the Conqueror," *National Geographic*, March 2000, p. 54.
3. Michael Wood, *In the Footsteps of Alexander the Great: A Journey from Greece to Asia.* Berkeley and Los Angeles: University of California Press, 1997, p. 22.
4. Quoted in John Maxwell O'Brien, *Alexander the Great: The Invisible Enemy, a Biography.* New York: Routledge, 1992, p. 6.
5. O'Brien, *Alexander the Great*, p. 6.
6. Plutarch, *Greek Lives: A Selection of Nine Greek Lives*, trans. Robin Waterfield. New York: Oxford University Press, 1998, p. 332.
7. A.B. Bosworth, *Conquest and Empire: The Reign of Alexander the Great.* New York: Cambridge University Press, 1988, p. 20.
8. Alexander, "Alexander the Conqueror," p. 54.
9. Plutarch, *Greek Lives*, p. 318.
10. O'Brien, *Alexander the Great*, p. 21.
11. Quoted in David Sacks, *A Dictionary of the Ancient Greek World.* New York: Oxford University Press, 1995, p. 2.
12. Sacks, *A Dictionary of the Ancient Greek World*, pp. 84–85.
13. Plutarch, *Greek Lives*, p. 313.
14. Wood, *In the Footsteps of Alexander the Great*, p. 24.
15. Plutarch, *Greek Lives*, p. 314.
16. O'Brien, *Alexander the Great*, p. 10.
17. Plutarch, *Greek Lives*, p. 315.
18. Plutarch, *Greek Lives*, p. 316.
19. Plutarch, *Greek Lives*, pp. 316–17.
20. Stoneman, *Alexander the Great*, p. 15.

Chapter 2: Inheriting His Father's Throne

21. Stoneman, *Alexander the Great*, p. 16.
22. Quoted in Ian Worthington, ed., *Alexander the Great: A Reader.* New York: Routledge, 2003, p. 59.
23. Peter Green, *Alexander of Macedon, 356-323 B.C.: A Historical Biography.* Berkeley and Los Angeles: University of California Press, 1991, p. 107.
24. Robin Lane Fox, *Alexander the Great.* New York: Dial, 1974, p. 24.
25. Alan Fildes and Joann Fletcher, *Alexander the Great: Son of the Gods.*

Los Angeles: J. Paul Getty Museum, 2001, p. 33.

26. O'Brien, *Alexander the Great*, p. 43.

27. J.R. Hamilton, *Alexander the Great*. Pittsburgh: University of Pittsburgh Press, 1973, p. 45.

28. Hamilton, *Alexander the Great*, p. 45.

29. Fox, *Alexander the Great*, p. 68.

30. Plutarch, *Greek Lives*, p. 323.

31. Fildes and Fletcher, *Alexander the Great*, p. 38.

32. Quoted in O'Brien, *Alexander the Great*, p. 53.

33. Quoted in Green, *Alexander of Macedon*, p. 145.

34. Arrian, *The Campaigns of Alexander*, trans. Aubrey de Sélincourt. New York: Dorset, 1971, p. 59.

35. Bosworth, *Conquest and Empire*, p. 33.

Chapter 3: Taking On the Persian Empire

36. Worthington, *Alexander the Great*, p. 45.

37. Hamilton, *Alexander the Great*, p. 50.

38. Pierre Briant, *Alexander the Great: Man of Action, Man of Spirit*. New York: Harry N. Abrams, 1996, p. 22.

39. Arrian, *The Campaigns of Alexander*, pp. 72–73.

40. Quoted in Briant, *Alexander the Great*, p. 43.

41. Fildes and Fletcher, *Alexander the Great*, p. 43.

42. Arrian, *The Campaigns of Alexander*, p. 75.

43. Arrian, *The Campaigns of Alexander*, pp. 757-76.

44. Quoted in Green, *Alexander of Macedon*, p. 181.

45. Green, *Alexander of Macedon*, p. 181.

46. Rick Black, "The March East: Alexander's Conquest of Asia and Egypt," *Calliope*, December 1998, p. 11.

47. Hamilton, *Alexander the Great*, p. 59.

48. Stoneman, *Alexander the Great*, p. 28.

49. Arrian, *The Campaigns of Alexander*, p. 82.

50. Hamilton, *Alexander the Great*, p. 59.

51. O'Brien, *Alexander the Great*, p. 68.

52. Stoneman, *Alexander the Great*, p. 31.

53. Arrian, *The Campaigns of Alexander*, p. 105.

54. Arrian, *The Campaigns of Alexander*, p. 112.

55. Quoted in Briant, *Alexander the Great*, p. 50.

56. Arrian, *The Campaigns of Alexander*, p. 123.

57. O'Brien, *Alexander the Great*, pp. 78–79.

58. Green, *Alexander of Macedon*, p. 235.

Chapter 4: "The King of All Asia"

59. Quoted in Arrian, *The Campaigns of Alexander*, p. 128.

60. O'Brien, *Alexander the Great*, p. 82.
61. Quoted in O'Brien, *Alexander the Great*, p. 83.
62. Bosworth, *Conquest and Empire*, p. 67.
63. Bosworth, *Conquest and Empire*, p. 68.
64. Plutarch, *Greek Lives*, p. 337.
65. Fildes and Fletcher, *Alexander the Great*, p. 59.
66. Quoted in Michael Grant, *Readings in the Classical Historians*. New York: Charles Scribner's Sons, 1992, p. 251.
67. Plutarch, *Greek Lives*, p. 339.
68. Quoted in Briant, *Alexander the Great*, p. 62.
69. Alexander, "Alexander the Conqueror," p. 65.
70. Green, *Alexander of Macedon*, pp. 295, 297.
71. Fildes and Fletcher, *Alexander the Great*, p. 66.
72. Quoted in Wood, *In the Footsteps of Alexander the Great*, p. 110.
73. Wood, *In the Footsteps of Alexander the Great*, p. 109.
74. O'Brien, *Alexander the Great*, p. 109.
75. Fildes and Fletcher, *Alexander the Great*, p. 79.

Chapter 5: Despot

76. Arrian, *The Campaigns of Alexander*, p. 182.
77. Briant, *Alexander the Great*, p. 80.
78. Fildes and Fletcher, *Alexander the Great*, p. 90.
79. Arrian, *The Campaigns of Alexander*, pp. 234–35.
80. A.B. Bosworth and E.J. Baynham, eds., *Alexander the Great in Fact and Fiction*. New York: Oxford University Press, 2000, p. 155.
81. Plutarch, *Greek Lives*, p. 154.
82. Arrian, *The Campaigns of Alexander*, p. 214.
83. Plutarch, *Greek Lives*, p. 361.
84. Quoted in Stoneman, *Alexander the Great*, p. 59.
85. Arrian, *The Campaigns of Alexander*, p. 226.
86. Green, *Alexander of Macedon*, p. 265.
87. Stoneman, *Alexander the Great*, p. 64.
88. Alexander, "Alexander the Conqueror," p. 72.
89. Quoted in Briant, *Alexander the Great*, p. 101.
90. Briant, *Alexander the Great*, p. 103.
91. Briant, *Alexander the Great*, p. 103.

Chapter 6: An Untimely Death and an Enduring Fame

92. Arrian, *The Campaigns of Alexander*, p. 336.
93. Arrian, *The Campaigns of Alexander*, p. 337.
94. Arrian, *The Campaigns of Alexander*, p. 339.
95. Hamilton, *Alexander the Great*, p. 163.
96. Quoted in Fildes and Fletcher, *Alexander the Great*, p. 147.
97. Plutarch, *Greek Lives*, p. 376.

98. Quoted in Stoneman, *Alexander the Great*, p. 81.

99. Quoted in Fildes and Fletcher, *Alexander the Great*, p. 58.

100. Arrian, *The Campaigns of Alexander*, p. 382.

101. Quoted in Ian Worthington, *Alexander the Great: Man and God*. New York: Pearson Education, 2004, p. 181.

102. Arrian, *The Campaigns of Alexander*, p. 393.

103. Arrian, *The Campaigns of Alexander*, p. 394.

104. Stoneman, *Alexander the Great*, p. 92.

105. Hamilton, *Alexander the Great*, pp. 34, 158.

For Further Reading

Books

Peter Chrisp, *Alexander the Great: The Legend of the Warrior King.* New York: Dorling Kindersley, 2000. A beautifully illustrated account of Alexander's life and times for young people.

Fiona MacDonald, *The World in the Time of Alexander the Great.* Philadelphia: Chelsea House, 2001. This book examines what was happening in other parts of the world during the conqueror's time as well as the major events in Alexander's life.

Gail B. Stewart, *Alexander the Great.* San Diego: Lucent, 1994. A clearly written and concise biography for young people.

Periodicals

Calliope, "Alexander the Great and the Spread of Greek Culture," December 1998. The entire issue of this history magazine for young people is devoted to Alexander and his legacy.

Web Sites

All About Alexander the Great: Alexander the Great's Home on the Web (www.pothos.org). A detailed and meticulously re-searched site on the conqueror and his times.

Ancient Greece (www.ancientgreece. com). Includes several excellent articles on Alexander the Great and much information on ancient Greek art, architecture, and mythology.

What's So Great About Alexander?: Greek Civilization for Middle Schoolers (www.historyforkids.org/ learn/greeks/history/hellenistic. html). An informative and entertaining site from Portland State University.

Works Consulted

Arrian, *The Campaigns of Alexander.* Trans. Aubrey de Sélincourt. New York: Dorset, 1971. Arrian's detailed account is one of the key ancient sources for Alexander's life and career.

A.B. Bosworth, *Conquest and Empire: The Reign of Alexander the Great.* New York: Cambridge University Press, 1988. An insightful biography of Alexander by one of the leading modern authorities on the conqueror.

A.B. Bosworth and E.J. Baynham, eds., *Alexander the Great in Fact and Fiction.* New York: Oxford University Press, 2000. A collection of essays on aspects of Alexander's career and legacy written by nine leading classical scholars.

Pierre Briant, *Alexander the Great: Man of Action, Man of Spirit.* New York: Harry N. Abrams, 1996. Includes numerous illustrations, maps, and diagrams and many fascinating details regarding the cultural world of Alexander the Great.

Alan Fildes and Joann Fletcher, *Alexander the Great: Son of the Gods.* Los Angeles: J. Paul Getty Museum, 2001. A beautifully illustrated biography intended for the general reader.

Robin Lane Fox, *Alexander the Great.* New York: Dial, 1974. A scholarly yet highly readable biography.

Michael Grant, *Readings in the Classical Historians.* New York: Charles Scribner's Sons, 1992. Includes selections from writings on Alexander by several classical historians, including the first-century-B.C. Greek historian Diodorus Siculus.

Peter Green, *Alexander of Macedon, 356–323 B.C.: A Historical Biography.* Berkeley and Los Angeles: University of California Press, 1991. A well-respected and absorbing biography.

J.R. Hamilton, *Alexander the Great.* Pittsburgh: University of Pittsburgh Press, 1973. Includes a helpful section on the major ancient sources for Alexander's life and times.

John Maxwell O'Brien, *Alexander the Great: The Invisible Enemy, a Biography.* New York: Routledge, 1992. An engrossing psychological profile of the conqueror.

Plutarch, *Greek Lives: A Selection of Nine Greek Lives.* Trans. Robin Waterfield. New York: Oxford University Press, 1998. Includes Plutarch's short biography of Alexander, one of the key early sources for the conqueror's life and career.

David Sacks, *A Dictionary of the Ancient Greek World*. New York: Oxford University Press, 1995. A helpful reference work that includes entries on places, persons, ideas, and events associated with the ancient Greek world.

Richard Stoneman, *Alexander the Great*. New York: Routledge, 1997. This concise biography includes a discussion of Alexander's achievements, both long- and short-term.

Michael Wood, *In the Footsteps of Alexander the Great: A Journey from Greece to Asia*. Berkeley and Los Angeles: University of California Press, 1997. A richly illustrated account of Alexander's life and of the author's own attempt to retrace the conqueror's path through western and central Asia more than two thousand years after his death. The book accompanies a four-part PBS television series of the same name.

Ian Worthington, *Alexander the Great: Man and God*. New York: Pearson Education, 2004. Includes a discussion of whether Alexander truly deserves the epithet "Great."

Ian Worthington, ed., *Alexander the Great: A Reader*. New York: Routledge, 2003. Includes excerpts from some of the most influential modern writings about Alexander.

Periodicals

Caroline Alexander, "Alexander the Conqueror," *National Geographic*, March 2000. Colorful photographs of ancient artifacts and of many of the places associated with Alexander enhance this article on the Macedonian conqueror.

Rick Black, "The March East: Alexander's Conquest of Asia and Egypt," *Calliope*, December 1998.

INDEX

PICTURE CREDIT

Cover: Alinari/Art Resource, N.Y.
AKG-Images/Peter Connolly, 41, 44, 75, 84
The Art Archive, 28, 60
Art Resource, N.Y. , 67
© Bettmann/CORBIS, 47, 71, 77, 83
© Sandro Vanni/CORBIS, 24
© Hulton Archive by Getty Images, 20
North Wind Picture Archives, 19, 35, 56, 65, 66
Stock Montage, Inc. 15, 18, 33, 53, 54, 86, 88, 90
Steve Zmina, 14, 25, 39, 52, 89

About the Author

Louise Chipley Slavicek received her master's degree in history from the University of Connecticut. She is the author often other books for young people, including *Life Among the Puritans, Confucianism*, and *Women of the American Revolution*. She lives in Ohio with her husband, James, a research biologist, and their two children, Krista and Nathan.